KNOCKHILL
50 YEARS OF RACING

KNOCKHILL
50 YEARS OF RACING

Stuart Gray

BLACK & WHITE PUBLISHING

First published in the UK in 2023 by
Black & White Publishing Ltd
Nautical House, 104 Commercial Street, Edinburgh, EH6 6NF

A division of Bonnier Books UK
4th Floor, Victoria House, Bloomsbury Square, London, WC1B 4DA
Owned by Bonnier Books
Sveavägen 56, Stockholm, Sweden

Text copyright © Stuart Gray 2023 and Knockhill Racing Circuit Ltd 2023
Photographs copyright © The Contributors, see page 253 for details

All rights reserved.
No part of this publication may be reproduced, stored or transmitted in any form
by any means, electronic, mechanical, photocopying or otherwise, without the
prior written permission of the publisher.

The right of Stuart Gray to be identified as Author of this work has been asserted
by him in accordance with the Copyright, Designs and Patents Act, 1988.

This book is a work of non-fiction, based on interviews about the lives, experiences and
recollections of its contributors. The publishers have made every effort to ensure that
the contents of this book are true to the best of their knowledge but cannot accept
responsibility for any information that may be incorrect.

The publisher has made every reasonable effort to contact copyright holders of images
and material used in this book. Any errors are inadvertent and anyone who for any reason
has not been contacted is invited to write to the publisher so that a full acknowledgement
can be made in subsequent editions of this work.

Cover design by Henry Steadman

Cover images copyright ©
Front cover: Flat Out Photography (left), Jim Moir (middle), Power Images (right);
Back cover, column one: V9 Photoworks (1), Dan Jess (2), Power Images (3), Knockhill Archives (4);
column two: Tom Brown (1), Tom Brown (2), V9 Photoworks (3);
column three: Power Images (1), Power Images (2), Jim Moir (3), Jim Moir (4)
Author photo: Cameron Robb

A CIP catalogue record for this book is available from the British Library.

ISBN: 978 1 78530 546 7

1 3 5 7 9 10 8 6 4 2

Layout by Richard Budd
Printed and bound in Lithuania

www.blackandwhitepublishing.com

This book is dedicated to the many employees, marshals, officials, medics, competitors and fans who have helped to create Knockhill over the years – thank you all.

Contents

viii	Foreword by David Coulthard
ix	A Word from the Champions
xi	Introduction

PART ONE
A Story of Three Owners

03	CHAPTER 1: The Tom Kinnaird Years One Man's Racing Vision
17	CHAPTER 2: The Derek Butcher Era Creating Scotland's National Motorsport Centre
31	CHAPTER 3: Jillian Shedden A Driving Force in a Changing World

PART TWO
Five Decades of Knockhill

45	CHAPTER 4: The First Decade The Challenging 1970s
71	CHAPTER 5: The Second Decade The Start of the Derek Butcher Era
91	CHAPTER 6: The Third Decade Developing Scotland's National Motorsport Centre
111	CHAPTER 7: The Fourth Decade Bringing New Events to Knockhill
131	CHAPTER 8: The Fifth Decade A Changing and Challenging Era for Motorsport

PART THREE
50 Years in Pictures

157	CHAPTER 9: Jim Moir 50 Years Through One Man's Lens
169	CHAPTER 10: Steven MacKay A Year in the Life of Knockhill
179	CHAPTER 11: Legends of Motorsport Snaps of Racing Stars
189	CHAPTER 12: Thrills and Spills And They Walked Away . . .
201	CHAPTER 13: Celebrity Visitors Guests from Stage, Screen and Sport

PART FOUR
Memorable Moments

209	CHAPTER 14: Did You Know? Top Trivia from the Track
225	CHAPTER 15: Fan's Favourites A Selection of Highlights
233	CHAPTER 16: Tales from the Tower Commentary Team Highlights
253	Acknowledgements and Image Credits
254	About Knockhill

Foreword
David Coulthard, MBE

Thirteen-time Formula 1 Grand Prix winner

Knockhill was the first race track where I drove a car. I was experienced in karting and so my father entrusted my development to the Leslies (father David and son David), and what a perfect decision that turned out to be! They used their contacts to source a year-old Van Diemen Formula Ford 1600 and their choice of race track wasn't one of the many English venues available. Instead, they chose Knockhill for me to learn what circuit racing was all about.

The track offered the perfect range of corners and topography for me to develop my skills. And that is why I am so happy to say happy birthday to Scotland's only permanent race track and thank you for everything that I learned while driving it.

David Coulthard, MBE
November 2023

A Word from the Champions

Jimmy McRae
Five-time British Rally Champion

The McRae family links with Knockhill stretch back almost forty years from when I competed in Scottish rallies and has continued with all of the McRaes at various times, right up to the 2022 McRae Rally Challenge and the naming of a corner at Knockhill as "McRae's corner".

Knockhill has played a vital role in Scottish motorsport since its inception, mainly hosting rallycross events in the early days, then being the venue for Super Special Stages of the Scottish Rally when I famously clashed with Dai Llewelyn going towards the loose section. I was not going to be second at my home track to a Welshman and that made the naming of that corner "McRae's corner" all the more of an honour for me!

My son Colin was a very regular visitor, often popping up to play with some of his cars and bikes, and he had a lot of fun with the Mk2 Escort and his superbikes, often with some of his British Superbike pals. With Alister living in Australia, his competitive drives at Knockhill have been few and far between, but it was great to see him win the first McRae Rally Challenge in 2015. And of course, Max, my grandson, is now rallying and is a regular too, and he passed his BARS rally licence test at Knockhill.

It has always been great to visit Knockhill, whether competing or recently as a spectator, whatever the weather, and I hope the circuit continues to go from strength to strength.

Niall Mackenzie
Ex-Grand Prix rider and three-time British Superbike Champion

It was a chance visit to Knockhill with school friends that landed me my lifelong obsession for motorcycle racing. Something inside told me I needed more than just spectating. Forty-three years on and, like so many motorsport fans, I still can't get enough of this remarkable circuit that has given my family decades of great memories.

A location that gives you views of the Wallace Monument and the three Forth Bridges is pretty special, but the magic lies within this special racetrack as it continues to produce world-class riders and drivers. With every type of corner and its undulating nature, it is perfect for youngsters learning skills and gives endless challenges to experienced competitors.

My professional racing career may have finished in 2000 but my involvement with Knockhill continues in many areas and I enjoy every visit just as much as that first day back in 1980. A huge congratulations to Derek and Jillian for their hard work and of course the loyal staff that have made these fifty years so successful. Over the years I've managed victories in seven separate classes at Knockhill, with many of these making my top ten special race day memories of my whole career. I am delighted that these are being featured later in this book too.

Time to raise a glass to the next fifty!

John Cleland
Two-time British Touring Car Champion

The very first visit I ever had to Knockhill was to drive a friend's Mini in a rallycross on 5 October 1975. I finished seventh overall but am not sure how many entered! After that, my reintroduction to Knockhill was when the British Touring Car Championships (BTCC) circus arrived in 1992.

I had just struck a deal with Derek Butcher to have Knockhill Racing Circuit on the visor of my crash helmet, which stayed there all through my BTCC career and around the world wherever I raced or tested.

The feeling at the circuit in those early days was of camaraderie and a can-do attitude that nothing was a problem, and every competitor had an exciting time and loved coming north. Given that it was the shortest lap time on the calendar, and with me being Scottish, I was always expected to do well at my "home" circuit. In reality, I won only one race during my BTCC career there and could never seem to get my driving style to dial into the circuit to achieve podium results. That only win was achieved during the 1993 BTCC race, by passing for the lead under braking for the hairpin and to this day I can still hear the noise of the capacity crowd as I did so!

Knockhill has built a reputation and a following of competitors over the years who will remember their days there fondly.

Introduction

On 22 September 1974, motorsport in Scotland changed forever with the opening of a new, purpose-built circuit on a hillside in Fife.

In the early 1970s, landowner Tom Kinnaird had the vision, with his friend Dave Brown, to create a permanent circuit on 200 acres of moorland he owned on the west side of the 1194-foot Knock Hill. So began his efforts to shape and carve out the profile of a racetrack. Its shape evolved, not through CAD/CAM designs or surveyors, but through his own imagination, using the shape of the terrain, an old railway line and threading between an existing army firing range and associated buildings.

Below: It was a keen photographer who ventured up Knock Hill to take a picture of the first race meeting.

The first bike meeting happened on 22 September 1974 with the circuit not yet having its final top surface of tarmac laid. Very shortly afterwards, Kinnaird was approached by businessman Denys Dobbie, who created a hugely ambitious five-year masterplan for Knockhill Racing Circuit, working with landowner Kinnaird to build a facility unlike anything else in Britain. The grand plan saw not only the 1.3-mile circuit extended to Grand Prix length, but also a massive multi-functional sports, leisure and accommodation complex.

However, the initial operators ran into immediate financial trouble with spiralling costs far outstripping expected revenues. The money ran out barely into the start of the planned building programme and so Tom Kinnaird took back control, buying the assets back from the administrators, and then leasing the venue out to several enthusiastic operators over the first ten years of the circuit. Without the certainty of a long-term lease arrangement, major capital investment was understandably not forthcoming from any of the annual tenants. But Knockhill survived this very shaky and vulnerable first decade.

Below: Scottish racers George Buchan (left) and Alastair King toasting the opening of the circuit on 22 September 1974 with the help of Irene Sinclair.

Opposite, top: And they're off! Bike racing was the most prominent activity in the early years at Knockhill.

Opposite, bottom: A newspaper article showing the additional Grand Prix extension that would go up Knock Hill, complete with elevation changes that would have been even more dramatic!

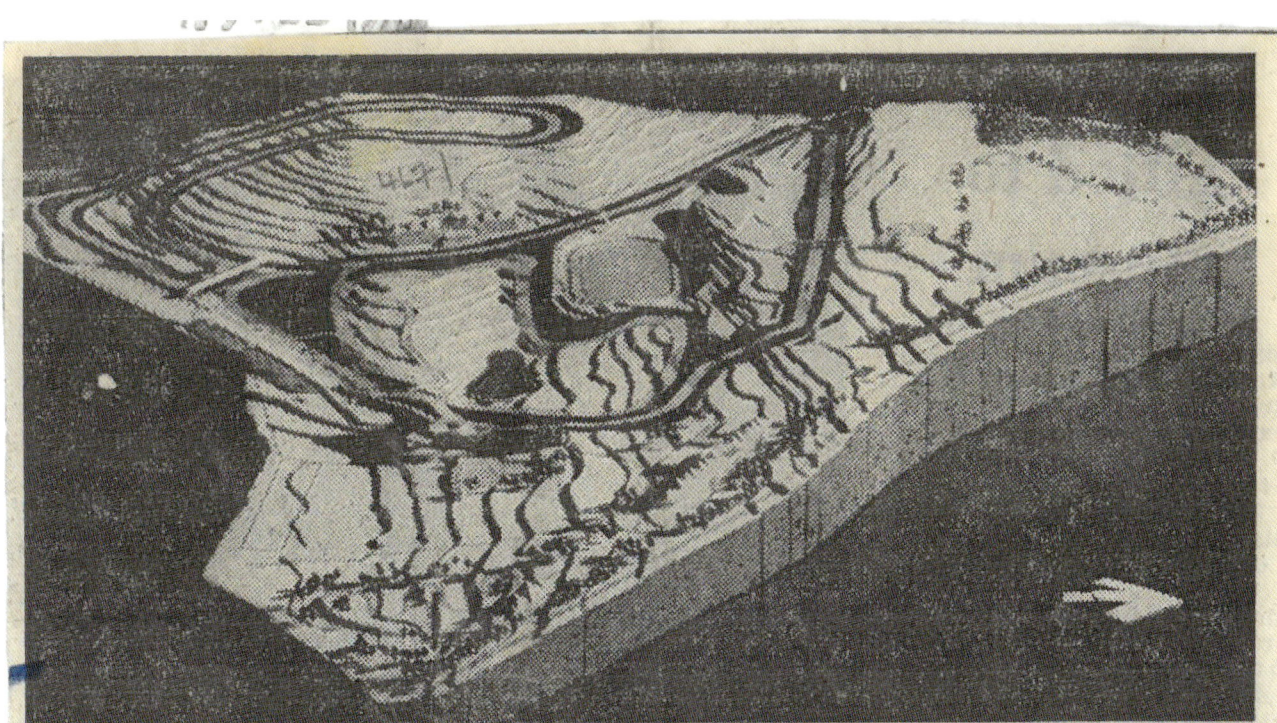

A model of the planned Knockhill Centre in Fife. Catering for many leisure pursuits, the centre is initially based on Knockhill motor racing circuit, and will cover some 200 acres.

Particular attention has been paid to the landscaping and design of the whole project so that features and building merge into the surrounding environment.

Ultimately the centre will have a hotel, touring caravan park, clubrooms, restaurant, go kart tracks, stadium, entertainment blocks and an international motor sport circuit.

Development will take approximately five years but during the development period an increasing volume of sporting activity will be arranged, starting with 25 meetings in 1975 covering motor cycle, karting, motor racing and rallycross.

It was not a until new owner, Derek Butcher, took the bold decision to buy Knockhill in September 1983 that things began to change. Derek and his team turned the almost facility-free, barren venue into Scotland's National Motorsport Centre. Over the next three decades it became known and highly regarded by many motorsport fans across the globe. This book traces the growth of Knockhill from those challenging early business years to becoming one of the foremost circuits in the UK and a regular venue for some of the top championships. What was Derek's secret to success? He says it was down to taking one step at a time and always reinvesting when finances allowed, ultimately achieving an FIA International Grade 3 Circuit Licence, the only one in the world licensed to run both clockwise and anti-clockwise, giving Scotland two top-class circuits at one venue.

Left: The opening event took place on a circuit that was barely ready. The kerbs were not complete and white lines had not been painted but the essence of the challenging track was there for all to enjoy.

The story is told through interviews with surviving Kinnaird family members, as well as Derek Butcher (who oversaw the development for almost forty years) and Jillian Shedden (the current owner who has had a life-long involvement and influence on the growth of the business from her early teenage years, before taking full control and ownership in February 2020). The interviews, anecdotes, words and pictures capture the essence of not only this unique and much-loved 1.3 miles of tarmac laid in the hills above Dunfermline in Fife, but also the business story behind its eventual success. Its undulating configuration with its own microclimate can be a challenge for all and it is often said that, "if you are fast and can win at Knockhill, then you can win at any circuit on the planet!" So it has proven, with many aspiring competitors learning their craft at Knockhill and going on to be champions on two, three and four wheels, not only in Scotland but Britain, Europe and throughout the world.

And so, this book covers Knockhill's first half-century and touches on what the next fifty years may hold. We hope you enjoy the read and admire the stunning photography from many of the UK's leading photographers who have gladly donated their work to this book; we are deeply grateful to them all. Many of the photos are in the archives of Knockhill and are not identified as to who took them, so our thanks to all listed and all those others not listed who have helped make *Knockhill: 50 Years of Racing* what it is.

Above: Karting was expected to be a main income stream for the circuit operations, as the sport was very strong in England. Sadly this did not transfer north of the border

Opposite, top: Club car racing completed the mix at Knockhill, meaning that the circuit was going head-to-head with major events at Ingliston Circuit. Here, two leading drivers of their time, Ian McLaren and Kenny Allen, battle it out.

Opposite, bottom: The mix of possibilities at Knockhill included Scotland's first purpose-built rallycross circuit, which would feature British Championship-level events from the outset.

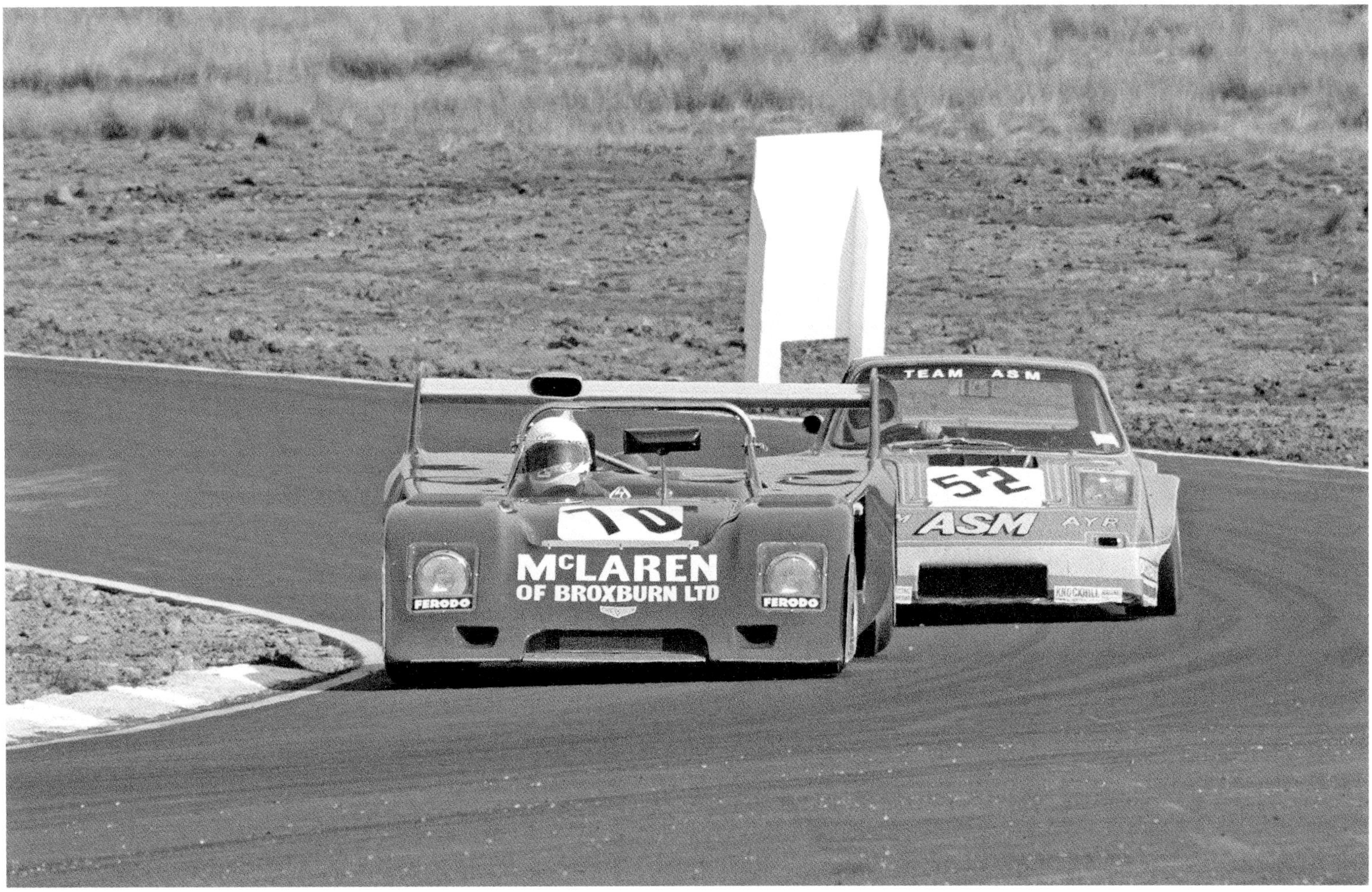
TEAM ASM
52
ASM
AYR
70
McLAREN
OF BROXBURN LTD
FERODO
FERODO

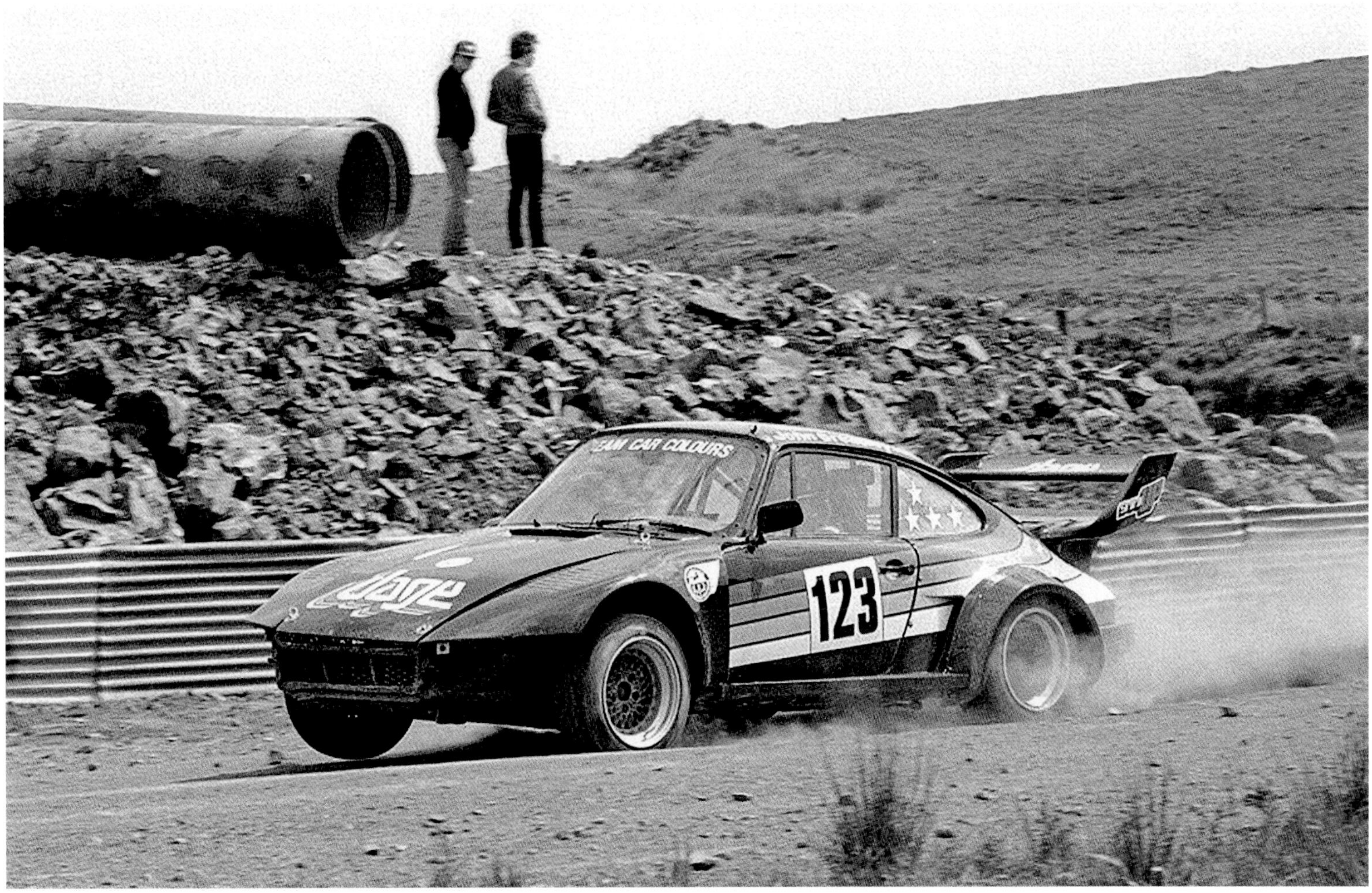
TEAM CAR COLOURS
123

PART ONE
A Story of Three Owners

Go-ahead for Knockhill plans

In spite of a report that Knockhill racing circuit is to close down, Dunfermline District Planning Committee yesterday gave the owner of the track, Mr Thomas Kinnaird, Cardenden, planning permission for some of the main buildings.

Director of Planning Mr Bill Shepherd said that his office had been in touch with Mr Kinnaird, who maintained that he still intended to operate the track.

Renewal of planning permission, until April 1983, was given for the existing circuit, offices and control building, on condition that certain improvements were made.

Permission was also granted for two new permanent buildings—a new spectators' stand, alterations to the commentators' box, and a new covered area for toilets, snack bar and storeroom with incorporated workshop.

"I am assured by Mr Kinnaird that he is keen to continue with the operation of the circuit, and it is hoped that the granting of these permissions will put the business on a more secure footing," Mr Shepherd said.

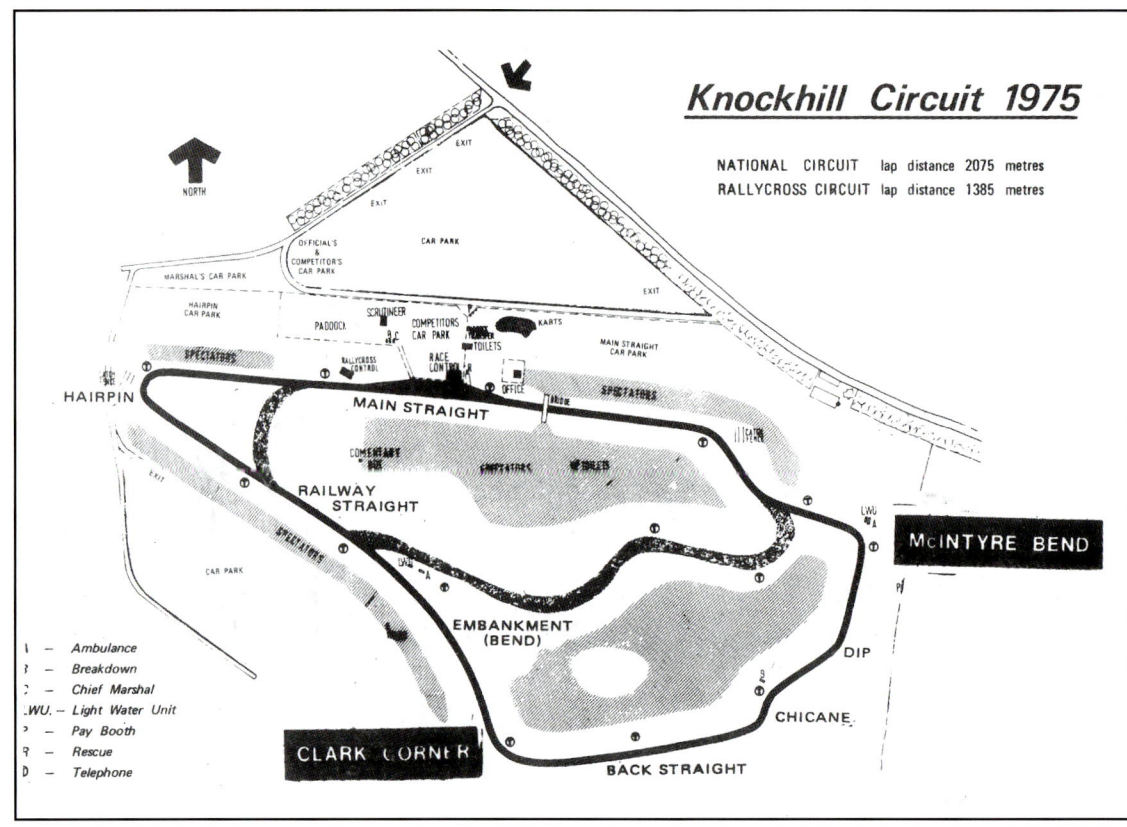

Above: A press cutting and circuit map from the 1970s.

Opposite: One of the earliest photos of a completed Knockhill circuit. The main features are the grass paddocks, a lack of any circuit buildings, the loch intended as a water sports centre, the old army range buildings at the chicane and the use of the old railway line to create the back straight from Clark's corner towards the hairpin.

Chapter 1
The Tom Kinnaird Years

One Man's Racing Vision

Above: A rare picture taken of Tom Kinnaird at a press event celebrating the resurfacing of the track. On the same day, the paddock restaurant was renamed Kinnairds in his honour.

Opposite, top left: An early picture of the chicane; how it's changed over the years to become one of the most iconic corners in British motorsport.

Opposite, top right: The ex-army Bailey Bridge that caused Tom Kinnaird a big headache with the local planners.

> What could be more appropriate for the United Kingdom, in perhaps its most financially difficult year yet, to have the RAC British Kart Championship for classes 210 and 250 at a bankrupt track. For, as seems to happen so often at new motor racing circuits around the world, the Scottish Knockhill track is now in the hands of the official receiver. Fortunately, anyone trying to turn such a piece of real estate into some form of going concern to pay even a percentage of the debts will inevitably find that there are precious few profitable alternatives to motorsport and that the upkeep is usually more costly if it is left idle than when being used. So, after a brief period of uncertainty, the Championships remained at Knockhill.
>
> However short of money the track may be, the surface, shape and situation are truly excellent and the spectators have a choice of excellent viewing areas including several perched high on cliffs that are the nearest thing to watching from the Goodyear Airship.

Karting Magazine, October 1976

After 1945, bike and car motorsport events in Scotland regularly used ex-RAF airfields such as Charterhall, Crimmond and Errol as they had become surplus to requirement after the war and had fresh tarmac or concrete laid. This made them ideal, along with their wide open spaces, long straights and plenty of room for paddocks. Jim Clark and Jackie Stewart were among the first to make their names at these venues, both in Scotland and throughout England.

The first purpose-built venue, however, was near Edinburgh Airport at Ingliston Racing Circuit, within the Royal Highland Showground, funded by a consortium of businessmen headed by John Romanes. As it was within the showground, it was ultimately a part-time racing venue as it would be returned to its primary use to host the Royal Highland Show every June. This would usually result in a six-race event schedule with three races from April, then three from August once the race infrastructure, barriers and other race equipment was replaced. The track was a challenge to look after and build as it was lined with Armco barriers, wending its way between numerous trees and buildings with around a mile of barriers to be erected, taken down and stored. Used exclusively by the Scottish Motor Racing Club, it became the sole Scottish venue for car sport featuring saloons, sports and Formula Ford 1600 and some mighty V8-engined ModSports/libre race cars. Some big names of the day raced at Ingliston including Doug Niven, Walter Robertson, Bill Dryden, Graham Birrell, George Franchitti, David Leslie and Ian Forrest, attracting sizeable crowds in the large, seated grandstands. Car racing was its core activity for many years; however, organisers did host both motorcycle and kart racing, but it was deemed too dangerous with the proximity of the barriers for further development of these disciplines.

Meanwhile, the Melville Motor Club had developed the high-speed, flat East Fortune Circuit in 1971 on a disused First World War airbase near Haddington. As a Scottish Auto Cycle Union-affiliated organisation, the Melville Club retains the circuit primarily as a motorcycle-only venue as additional car-related activity has been rendered impossible owing to restrictions imposed by nearby residential development and the fact that the surface was protected to preserve its Second World War history.

With the tight and twisty nature of Ingliston, and cars becoming faster and faster, the motor racing scene in Scotland needed something to happen, as the Edinburgh venue was severely limited by the nature of its layout and impediments to further development imposed by its landlords, the Royal Highland Society.

The change came from an unlikely source: Fife potato merchant, sheep farmer and businessman Tom Kinnaird at South Lethans, a 200-acre farm on the side of Knock Hill, some 5 miles north of Dunfermline. Tom's vision was to build his own circuit. With business partner David Brown, he formed the Knockhill Development Company and worked on the project for three years from 1971 before construction started, investing some £80,000. The track evolved, not through computer aided design or professional consultants, but rather with imagination, instinct and a healthy dose of common sense and pragmatism. Using the shape of the terrain, the track bed of a disused coal mine railway and an ex-Army firing range service road with its associated buildings, Tom's dream began to be realised in the form of an undulating 1.3 mile circuit.

When the Mid Argyll Motor Club hosted the very first bike meeting in September 1974, incoming spectators meant there was traffic chaos for miles around. Fife Police were not impressed! Although facilities were very basic and the track did not even have its final sealed-top tarmac surface, there were plans, even then, to develop and extend the circuit and create more facilities. In the spirit of the times, the circuit was officially opened with a "champagne shower" by former Scots racing stars Alastair King and George Buchan on the start line with a bottle of bubby being wielded by Irene Sinclair, one of three Argyll Club girls dressed in tartan miniskirts for the occasion.

> Welcome to this historic inaugural race meeting at Knockhill, Scotland's first and only motorsport complex. You are present today at the fulfilment of a dream. For decades, every true motorsport enthusiast in Scotland has yearned for a permanent circuit "home" where racing never had to take second place to other activities. Now this wish has been granted for us all by Mr Thomas Kinnaird and Mr Brown whose three years of work has produced at, a cost of £80,000, this 1.3-mile circuit set among the finest scenery of any track in Britain. During the next twelve months, at least another £100,000 will be spent on pit, paddock, changing room, clubroom, grandstand and – most exciting of all – an extension of the course to 2.25 miles.
>
> Competitors who have tried the circuit say that Knockhill is as well thought-out as any course in Britain. It will take some learning to go round really fast. What racing men have praised is the space. For those who can't avoid trouble there is plenty of run-off area – without any Armco barriers. Spectator safety is assured by the absence of viewing areas on the outside of turns. From a central reservation inside the course, it is possible to watch almost an entire lap.

Motor Cycle Road Racing at Knockhill Race Circuit on

Sunday 22nd September 1974

FIRST RACE – 1.00 p.m.

WARNING TO THE PUBLIC

MOTOR RACING IS DANGEROUS and spectators attending at this track do so **ENTIRELY AT THEIR OWN RISK**. It is a condition of admission that all persons having any connection with the promotion and/or organisation and/or conduct of the meeting, including the owners of the land and the drivers and owners of the vehicles are absolved from all liability arising out of accidents causing personal injury, whether fatal or otherwise, to ticket holders or **SPECTATORS** or their property.

OFFICIAL PROGRAMME – 15p.

THE CENTRE

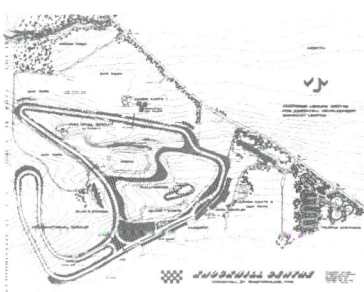

The proposed Knockhill Centre will be developed on a 80-hectare (200 acres) site, 16 km. north of the Forth Bridge in the County of Fife, Scotland. On the eastern fringe of an area zoned as being of great landscape value, the site is situated close to the M90 and within 30 minutes' drive of Edinburgh on the approaches to the Scottish Highlands. Readily accessible to the main centres of population in Scotland and based initially on racing activities with a purpose-built circuit, the Centre will provide top-quality facilities for all aspects of motor sport and for the first time allow Scottish Formula 1 drivers and super-bike riders to compete in International events before home crowds. Sport and extensive leisure facilities will also be provided on site to cater for visitors and local needs at present lacking in this part of Scotland.

An extensive Landscaping and planting programme will integrate the development with the surrounding countryside.

The five-year development plan aims to provide unique facilities for motor sport, motor-cycle racing, rallycross, karting, stock-car racing, etc. and hotel, club, caravanning and leisure pursuits. Excellent national air links are available less than 30 km. from Knockhill.

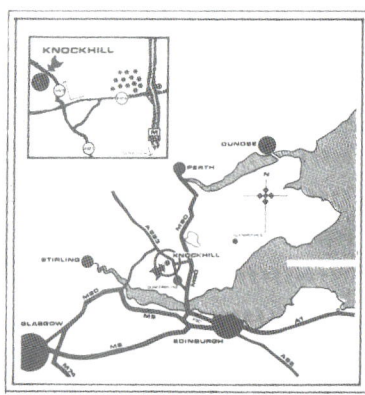

All in all, the motorsport fan has plenty to look forward to in the way of thrills and entertainment at Knockhill. The racing will be hard, make no mistake about that. Every circuit sorts the men from the boys after its own fashion. Knock Hill, with its swirling twists and gradients, will sort them out particularly well.

Competitors – the best of luck to every one of you. Enjoy your racing and keep within your limits. Spectators – may you enjoy this first day out at Knockhill and come again for more.

We look forward to welcoming you all, with your family and friends, at the first Knockhill event of 1975.

The Directors of the Knockhill Development Company

Opposite: The cover and welcome page of the first events programme at Knockhill.

Above: Sidecars have always been a mainstay of racing activity from the outset. Leading sidecar racers included John Bottomley (3), Iain Dickie (24) and Alister Lewis (2), all seen competing here.

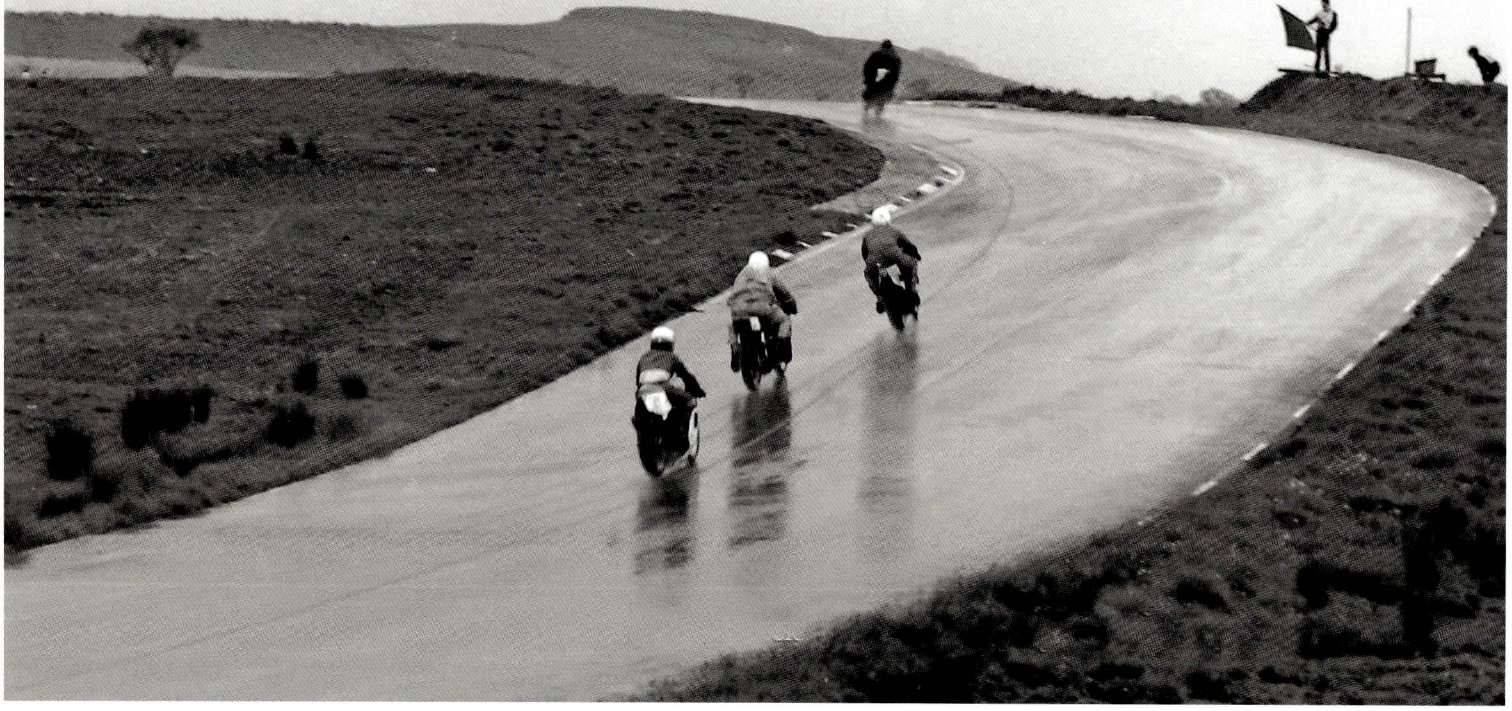

Above: In the early days at Knockhill, the owners couldn't afford enough white paint to define the track edges – so a dotted line was painted instead!

Below and opposite: Knockhill certainly made all the national press as the bold plans included a Grand Prix sized circuit for Scotland.

A blustery over-cast sky does not flatter Knockhill. Pictured here, part of the (when photographed) partially completed track and run-off verging.

Knockhill: Scotland's chance for a big-time motor racing circuit

By IAN SADLER **Photographs by PETER NEWTON**

The name of Knockhill is one that should become familiar to a large cross-section of motor sport participants in seasons to come. It doesn't sound very much like a motor racing track but that is what it is; and a very significant new name it should turn out to be. Driving up the winding road towards Knockhill there isn't, yet, very much to see, apart from the attractive climb into the hills. You can tell that there is something going on, perhaps the Forestry Commission or the Water Board, but once inside the perimeter fence you are left with no doubt that Knockhill is an embryo race track: Caterpillars squeaking on their tracks, rollers, dumpers, mud everywhere and a smooth black ribbon of asphalt. From the portable cabins, the temporary headquarters, you can shelter from the bitter March wind and study most of the "National" designated circuit taking form. The track is laid and a super-smooth layer has, just this week, been completed. As Knockhill's chairman and managing director, Denys Dobbie, said during our visit: "Most of the work here has been in getting the ground ready — it is only now beginning to look like a race track."

Knockhill began in 1972 with the 750 Motor Club of Dundee and an oil company sponsor getting together to plan a little track, principally a rallycross circuit. Things proceeded shakily at first but since Denys Dobbie took hold of the reins late last year, the Knockhill plans have been entirely revised and now — with an expenditure of more than £300,000 — the circuit is fast taking shape. Knockhill is not to be anything resembling its low-key beginnings. Now, it is a highly significant, totally new, venture for British motor racing: a custom-built "complex" from scratch.

Denys Dobbie could be described as an "arch enthusiast." A wealthy man, Dobbie has been a part of the racing scene for a number of years, starting with his own team of two Chevron B16 sports cars for Graham Birrell and John Miles. The DART (Dobbie Automobile Racing Team) cars for '72 were B19s. Since then Dobbie has had an association with the Rondel team and was director of GRD for a year, with cars (F3 and 2 litre sports) for Alan Jones and Dave Walker. Dobbie's links with racing have been of a successful and substantially respected nature and now, with Knockhill, Denys Dobbie is taking his involvement to much higher stakes and the rewards can [illegible] is, until you find out about the rest of the complex.

Knockhill's plans encompass a five-year programme, the first phase of which is to establish the circuit for car and motor cycle racing and put the rallycross track into full activity. Both of these facilities are on target for this year; the rallycross circuit already in operation (and well sorted since their first "mudbath" meeting — see **Sports Extra**. Just last week Basil Tye gave the 1.35 mile national circuit the RAC's blessing, with very little additional work to be required before the first action.

Safety first

Being a fresh design from the outset Knockhill has safety paramount, the entire track having a substantial run-off area with layers of catch fencing and Armco in all the strategic places. Notable features include a generously sized and properly surfaced paddock and a large and easily controlled pits area with a substantial slip road onto and off the track. Of the track itself, the crux of the operation—the layout appears to be both imaginative and exciting. For that number-one requirement — spectators, Knockhill can boast a natural amphitheatre with its "in the hills" location and there appear to be several prime vantage points, either for watching almost all of the circuit at a single view, or for nestling, safely, close-in to the corners. Either way, there are no blind spots for the public.

The excitement will come from the competitors just as soon as racing speeds are attained. Touring around in a saloon, dodging in and out of the plant, little imagination is needed to envisage where the action will be. There are several stretches where driving talent will bring quick laps, and anything less would have the driver on quite the wrong line and heading for the boondocks. It is definitely a

Knockhill's dynamo — chairman and managing director Denys Dobbie.

driver's circuit. Indeed, at a couple of places, Timo Makinen would feel almost "at home," with a fast left-right over a rising and blind crest, where the car will make a transition from positive down G to very, very light within the space of an eye-blink. There is also a hairpin which must have been considered the circuit designer's secret weapon. Slowing from a high speed on a slightly tightening radius curve, the dog-leg right looms much tighter than it looks and without the benefit of much assisting camber either. This corner is one of the sections quite rightly ear-marked for triple catch-fence.

The programme at Knockhill is for much more than just providing Scotland with another tiddler circuit to complement Ingliston. The nine metres wide track will allow all forms of motor racing up to Formula 2 and plans are in gear for an extension to 3.7 km for a truly international circuit. The current 20 pits will increase to 40 and nothing less than a Scottish Grand Prix is the ultimate aim. The 2.1 km track will be finished in the near future and national status meetings will be held later this year. Knockhill will also be fully suited to motor cycles and a series of dates for this year includes an international trophy weekend and a super-bike championship. Scrambles and trials facilities will also be made available. The permanent rallycross circuit is already in operation and this will be used in conjunction with other loose and tar tracks for a rally drivers' school. The facility will be sharing classrooms with a racing drivers' school.

Not being forgotten, Karts will also enjoy the circuit and the UK National Championships are scheduled to take place at Knockhill. For 1976 there will also be a twistier 800 metre track for Class 1 Karts, the location entirely in view from the main racing grandstands. Furthering the diverse programme will be a multi-purpose arena (within a natural terraced amphitheatre) which will house a 400 metre circuit for speedway and stock cars. Trotting, show jumping and other activities and festivals will be catered for as the calendar allows.

"We want Knockhill on the international map—nothing short of this will suffice"—Denys Dobbie

Under the broad heading of "leisure" is where Knockhill should accelerate beyond any defined motor sport limits. Encompassed in the five-year programme are plans, to be franchised out, for a whole spectrum of leisure facilities. Knockhill will eventually boast a leisure and entertainments' centre to be constructed adjoining the racing circuit grandstands. There will be a central development featuring a sports hall, swimming pool, sauna, squash and multi-purpose halls. A 200-bedroom international class hotel will be built on the northern slopes, all of the building kept to a two-storey height. Complementing the hotel will be a country club, destined for the Western hillside, with dancing, dining and cabaret plus limited luxury accommodation, providing a base for those wishing to fish, shoot and enjoy golf as well as serving the centre.

Knockhill have published expected commencement dates for their wide-ranging and ambitious programme. These include the following priorities: Motor Racing to F2 level, mid-1975 (international F2, 1976); Racing drivers school, skidpan, rallycross, Kart racing on car circuit, 1975. Motor Racing up to F1 International, mid-'79. Scrambling, trials, motor cycle racing, 1975. Picnic Area and caravan site, 1975. Leisure pursuits mid-1978; hotel and function suite, mid-'78.

As can be read into the above, Knockhill is planned to be a very major circuit for future British motor racing. Once all the sundry building and enlargement is completed, the Knockhill complex could well become the venue for the first ever International Scottish Grand Prix.

The fervour and enthusiasm with which plans are being executed bodes well for this dream circuit to come true.

The location

At the moment Knockhill could be described as "on the bleak side"; however, the hilly nature of the location should allow a "good" day to be enjoyed to the full; a bad day will be more enduring for spectators, though, as more satellite facilities are constructed, less so. Access is easy with the M90 motorway from Edinburgh, just four miles distant. Time from Turnhouse Airport should be around 30 minutes. The nearest large town is Dunfermline, a few miles south of the location, though by mid-'78 Knockhill should be largely self-sufficient.

The action already takes place here — a view of the revised and fast rallycross course.

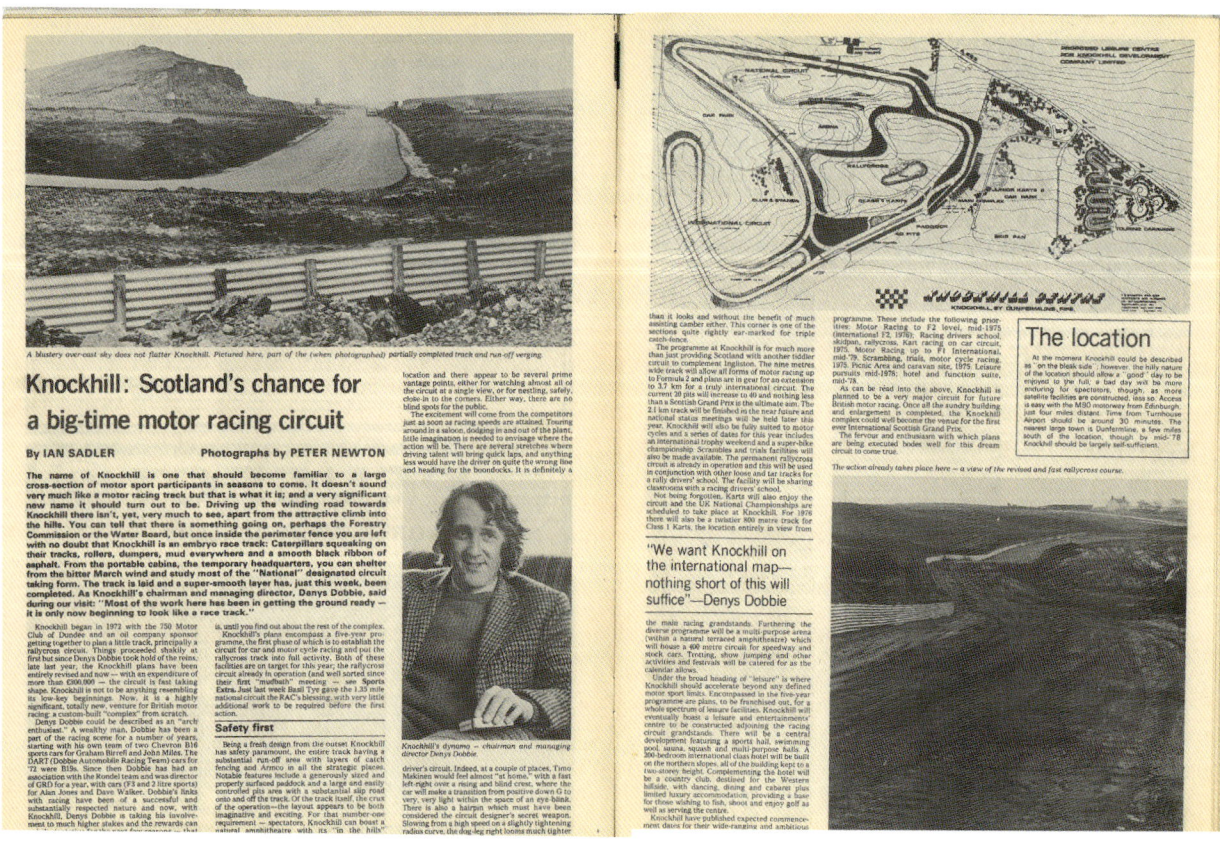

AUTOSPORT — A Haymarket publication — 10 April 1975 18p

SAFARI REPORT – DIJON 1000 – KNOCKHILL PLANS

Full report of dramatic Circuit of Ireland

Dobbie backs Scot circuit

Denys Dobbie, the man behind the DART racing projects of recent years, has taken over as chairman of Knockhill Development Co to increase the pace of building and construction work on Scotland's new racing circuit.

Already progress has been made on the circuit which is between Edinburgh and Perth and it is hoped that RAC approval will be forthcoming in the next two weeks for a rallycross meeting to be held later this year. It is hoped for a full programme of events, motor and motor cycle racing, to be held next year.

● Despite ambitious plans in Italy, GRD fortunes have taken a tumble with the news that their Italian importer Renato Monzeglio suffered a heart attack soon after the press announcement.

AUTOSPORT, OCTOBER 31, 1974

Dobbie buys out Knock Hill

DENYS DOBBIE, the man who formed the DART racing team in 1970, has bought a controlling interest in Knock Hill, the new Scottish circuit being built in Fifeshire. This seems to be about the best thing that could have happened to the half-completed Knock Hill track, for it will bring just the infusion of capital that the project needed. David Brown remains as managing director of the Knock Hill Development Company, however.

Dobbie plans to develop the site as an all-round recreation centre, not just a racing circuit, and wants to have racing and rally drivers' schools at the venue. There are also tenuous plans to build a further loop onto the existing layout, bringing the track up to full international standard within the next five years.

Last week Denys Dobbie visited the 1.4-mile circuit which is situated halfway between Dunfermline and Crieff. With him was his former number one driver in the DART team, John Miles. Borrowing Bill Dryden's Firenza, they drove round the spectacular course, which already has a tarmac surface although the top dressing has still to be applied, and John made one or two suggestions for minor improvements. The venue has yet to receive the RAC's blessing for car racing (a motor bike meeting has already been held), but that is expected within the next couple of weeks.

Before starting the DART team in 1970, Dobbie a Scotsman, was himself a club racer, first at Charterhall and then in the Bahamas. DART began by entering Graham Birrell, but achieved its greatest successes with John Miles in 2-litre sportscar racing.

£3m Grand Prix track for Scotland

MOTOR RACING by Mervyn Edgecombe

AN ambitious £3 million plan to revive motor sport in Scotland is being engineered by a millionaire ex-racing driver.

He is developing a one-time muddy circuit at Knockhill, Dunfermline, into motor sport's answer to the Aviemore winter sports complex.

It will be ready by 1980, when stockbroker Denys Dobbie is hoping to stage the British Grand Prix there.

He has already established Scotland's first rallycross circuit at Knockhill, staging British and European championship events.

Eventually the mile-and-a-half racing circuit — where Formula Two events are now held — will be extended to almost four miles and widened to take Formula One.

Forty pits are to be built to bring the circuit to international standards and planning permission has been given for a big hotel and a country club.

Scotland on the international motor map.

'And Knockhill, I'm confident, will do that. We shall cater for every kind of motoring interest.

'There are perfect rallying facilities, with tarmac, asphalt, and loose driving surfaces at the 200-acre complex and it is planned to set up a rallycross school there.

Mr. Dobbie, 37, who once ran the Dart racing team, said: 'I want to put One world champion Emmerson Fittipaldi and his brother Wilson to visit the course for meetings later this year.

'I know there is the support and interest up here, so I'm going all out to tap it. I'm very confident,' he added.

KNOCKHILL —
1975 @ RALLYCROSS, JAN. 5

The new Knockhill Race Circuit at Saline in Fife will launch Motor Sport 1975 on January 5 with Scotland's first ever full-blooded Rallycross.

With a total of £750 offered in awards, interest has already been considerable. The organisation will be in the hands of Thames Estuary Automobile Club in conjunction with the East Ayrshire DC and Lanarkshire DC and the 750 MC (Scotland).

TEAC are experienced in this type of event and, in association with the other clubs, will run another four main meetings covering the first four months of the year. There are eight scheduled for the whole year. First ten in each of three runs will share in the prize money which will give greater encouragement.

Regulations can be had from: K.S. Kaye, TEAC, 167 Bentleet Road, Benfleet, Essex, or Denys Dobbie, Knockhill Circuit, Saline, nr. Dunfermline, Fife.

RAPID PROGRESS

Headed by Chairman Denys Dobbie of the Knockhill Development Co. and ably assisted by managing director David Brown, one of the founders of the project, and fellow director, Cupar lawyer, Dermont McCarroll, rapid progress has been made in getting the circuit knocked into shape for the coming 75 season. While car, motor cycle and kart sport will be the prime interest, the longer term plan is to develop the 200-plus acre site as a leisure centre incorporating many compatible leisure activities.

Mr. Dobbie, Scots business man and lifelong motor sport enthusiast and owner of the successful DART racing team, believes Knockhill will become the centre of motor sport in Scotland. Mr. David Brown is supervising circuit construction and improvements. Full circuit car racing, given the RAC's blessing, should be a fact by June, 1975.

A great deal of work has been done in constructing wide run-off areas on either side of the track and many hundreds of yards of steel sheet barrier have been erected for competitor and spectator safety.

CIRCUIT BASED

Five kart race meetings, for 250cc machines are scheduled. On the motor cycle side, the parent company is in the course of forming a circuit-based club known as the Knockhill Motor Cycle Racing Club who will promote all forms of motor cycle sport at the circuit, in co-operation with other interested motor cycle clubs — the administration of events being similar to the successful groups in England. Affiliation of the new club has been applied for to the Scottish Auto-Cycle Union.

The Rallycross track uses much of the tarmac surface but cuts through the inside and by-passes a small loch before rejoining the racing circuit again.

On Circuit With . . .
JACK DAVIDSON

A recent visit to Knockhill, which has excellent spectating points, sees the racing start on a pretty short straight followed by a 50 degree right hand bend which leads into a fast sweeping left-hander.

A long straight comes next ending

Scottish Clubman

with a beautifully cambered hairpin to the right. Then on to another straight, this time up and over a hill, where the light single seaters 'yump' over the brow.

Here is the start of the Rallycross circuit. After hitting the top of the hill there is a 90 degree downhill right bend followed by a left at the bottom. A short straight leads to another 90 degree right-hander, another short straight followed by yet another 90 degree right.

The next short straight ends on a steep upward climb at a 90 degree left round the back of a firing range and immediately sharp right round the outside of a hut to the finish.

MOTORING TODAY

Car sport centre planned for Knockhill

BY A MOTORING CORRESPONDENT

The Knockhill circuit, which opened at the beginning of the year near Glenrothes, Fife, has got away to a flying start in more ways than one.

Apart from the rallycross event which christened the circuit, the organisers, Knockhill Ltd. announced today that planning permission has been granted for a 200-acre centre based on the racing circuit, which will include a touring caravan park, clubrooms, restaurant, go-kart tracks, stadium, entertainment blocks, and an international motor sport circuit.

Development, according to the organisers, will take five years, but during the development period an increasing volume of sporting activity will be arranged, starting with 25 meetings in the current year covering motor cycle, karting, motor racing, rally-cross.

Next year the variety and leisure activity will be expanded to cover athletics and equestrian events.

An example of the variety of sporting opportunities which may result directly or indirectly from Knockhill was seen late last month when the Scottish Sporting Car Club held their Grand Prix de Knockhill. This was won by Chris Merrick, from an entry of 32, most of whose cars had to be bodily lifted back on to the correct route during the race, and lasted over two hours — even though it was an event for electrically driven model cars on a model course.

✦ ✦ ✦

FROM TODAY there will be a new, and potentially significant name in British motoring — Polski-Fiat.

Arrangements for the import of the Italian-designed, Polish-built cars have now been finalised, and they will join the Russian Ladas in April as strong contenders for a market in which Eastern European versions of the highly successful Italian products are already well represented.

The agreement has been signed between Pol-Mot, the Foreign Trade Enterprise for the Polish Automotive Industry, and Polski Car Imports (GB) Ltd., a new British company. Polski Car will become concessionaires for Polski-Fiat in the UK.

The new company which will be controlled by Mr. John Ebenezer as managing director, utilises the same board and management team which at present looks after the interests of the Japanese Mazda and East German Wartburg vehicles.

✦ ✦ ✦

THE SCOTTISH Sporting Car Club's Starlight Rally will take place on March 8 and 9, over a 160-mile course, starting at a Lochwinnoch garage and ending at a Giffnock hotel. The event will consist of two classes, one open to any competitor and the other for non-experts. The minimum entry for the event will be 35 and the maximum 90, including reserves. Entry list closes on March 3.

The club's Moonbeam Rally was held at the end of last month, and the result, over a course starting from Newhouse Garage, resulted in a win for David Black and Ross Finlay in a VW 1302S.

Since Ross is a fellow journalist, it is a double pleasure to record that he not only carried out faultless instruction over the route which ended at the Angus Hotel, Hamilton, but also won a navigational test at the end by two seconds from his nearest competitor.

An interesting entrant at that first meeting, and a taste of what was to come in the future, was rider number 17 in the programme, a Mr D Butcher from Burntisland, who entered three bikes, a 200cc, 350cc and a 1000cc.

Not long after that first bike meeting, Tom was approached by DART Formula 3 team owner, and highly successful Perth businessman Denys Dobbie to lease the circuit and as early as 31 October, just five weeks after the opening event, the following was reported in *Motoring News*:

> "Dobbie had bought a controlling interest in Knockhill, the new Scottish circuit being built in Fifeshire. This seems to have been the best thing that could have happened to the half-completed Knockhill track, for it will bring the infusion of capital that the project needed. David Brown remains as Managing Director of the Knockhill Development Company, however."

He created an even grander five-year masterplan for Knockhill to build a facility unlike anything else in Britain and by 8 November 1975 it was reported in the local press that Dobbie had formed the Knockhill Development Company Limited, of which he was chairman, supported by David Brown, one of the original movers in the project, and Cupar lawyer Dermott McCarroll. After hosting a bike meeting, the venue had yet to be granted a car racing licence from the RAC MSA, the governing body of car sport in the UK. Despite that, his ambitious ideas intended that the 1.3-mile circuit be extended to incorporate a 2.25-mile Grand Prix circuit. Additionally, he planned a 200-bed international-class hotel with a sports complex, swimming pool, sauna, multi-purpose halls, a caravan park, leisure and pony-trekking centres and more. In an article in *Autosport*, Dobbie claimed he would invest some £300,000 (equivalent to around £4 million in today's money). In the *Press and Journal* of 1975, on 24 February, it was reported that Dobbie would expand further to incorporate athletics and equestrian events and that shopping and restaurant facilities would be built too. They would host twenty-five meetings a year including motorcycles, karting, motor racing and rallycross, and crowds of 10,000 would attend such national events.

Dobbie's grand vision was to have a venue that could host the first-ever International Scottish Grand Prix. Forty pit garages would be built and large grandstands, too, allowing international Formula 1 events followed by a Scottish Grand Prix the year after. At that time, Scottish motorsport was still ringing to the achievements of the late Jim Clark as well as the profile and successes of Sir Jackie Stewart. Two world champions from a tiny nation created a feeling that Scotland could easily punch above its weight when it came to racing – whether that was on two wheels, three or four!

Opposite: At the official opening of the circuit in 1975 for car racing, New Zealand F5000 star Chris Amon is seen cutting the ribbon at the official opening of the circuit in 1975 for car racing.

Below: Rounding Railway bend having exited Clark's, Chris Amon demonstrates his Talon F5000 at Knockhill's opening car race meeting.

Chapter 1: The Tom Kinnaird Years

The first car event at the circuit was actually a rallycross, using both the tarmac and loose section through the centre of the venue on Sunday 5 January 1975. In hindsight, it was a highly optimistic move to run such an event in the middle of the winter. A series of rallycross events were scheduled for 1975 as, at that time, car racing was the premier activity at Ingliston. The realisation as to the challenges that lay ahead must have struck home rapidly as the event did not end well; only two of the three planned runs for the competitors could be completed owing to the loose section turning into a mud bath. Cars were getting stuck and were not powerful enough to drive a complete lap without getting bogged down. The eventual winner was Englishman David Potter, who won the lion's share of the £750 prize money, and he drove south £150 better off. Potter was competing in a Mini with Scotsman John Gemmell finishing second in an Avenger GT.

The headlines in the press were not kind about the abandonment of the meeting, with headlines such as "Mud Galore as rallycross arrives", "Milling about in the mud", "Mud bath at Knockhill", "Wind and mud mar rallycross meeting at new Fife circuit" and "Knockhill rallycross meeting cancelled". Later, Dobbie claimed a mechanical digger had fractured the main drain, causing the mud bath and that it would be fixed for the series of rallycross events that were scheduled in his first season, the next of which was in March. This first car event was run by TEAC, the Thames Estuary Automobile Club, who had links with Lydden Hill in Kent, in association with the 750 Motor Club, Lanarkshire and East Ayrshire Motor Clubs.

Above: The winner of the first car race was Edinburgh's Eddie Labinjoh.

Below: The 1976 Indylantic race starts with wannabe Formula 1 drivers on the grid.

Adding to the mix of bike meetings and rallycross, Dobbie had identified kart race meetings as a key line of activity at Knockhill. A six-event programme had been earmarked for 1975 and it was intended to give "the Fife circuit its biggest ever boost". Dobbie had approached well-known English karting impresario Brian Hesketh of the Morecombe and Heysham Club to organise the meetings, the first of which was planned for 4 May. But the challenges of running meetings were evident as even before the karting season event in March, the media across Scotland were running pleas for volunteer marshals to come forward otherwise the events would not go ahead. An advert in March 1975 read:

> **Marshals needed! The new Scottish racing circuit at Knockhill, Fife, needs a team of enthusiastic marshals. 200 volunteer officials must be found from the ranks of Scottish motorsport clubs before the first meeting – scheduled for 18 May – can take place.**

Dobbie's ambitions seemed out of step with the reality of motorsport in Scotland. Certainly he appeared to have the funds and he did not do things by half as he continued his grand plan for his first full season. In March 1975 he had claimed in the national press that he would be spending £3 million on the complex in his five-year plan (some £20 million in today's money).

To start with a showcase event, he would invite, and pay, a high-profile driver of the time, Chris Amon, to officially open the circuit with a tape-cutting ceremony. Chris would drive his Talon F5000 as part of this first event.

Lapping in 54.1 seconds, Amon's car was an impressive sight, and sound, for all those present, including a young Bo'ness photographer Jim Moir. Moir had photographed the opening bike event and would go on to attend events for the next fifty years. (His work will be seen throughout the book and he has his own chapter about the changes in motorsport photography and camera technology.) That first event was well attended, had good weather and was run by the Lothian Sports Car Club. Edinburgh businessman Eddie Labinjoh, a regular racer at Ingliston, had the honour of winning the first-ever car race in his Alfa Romeo 2000 GTV, from Ian Smith in a Mazda and Tom Meldrum in a Ford Escort Mexico.

Later in the summer, a selection of aspiring Formula 3 drivers were invited north, including American drivers Danny Sullivan and a seventeen-year-old Eddie Cheever, for what was hoped to be a money-spinner for Dobbie, as sponsorship had also been found. There were some challenges for those racers as the promised start money did not materialise and there were threats of cars being put back on trailers and not racing. But a deal was struck, and the event proceeded, but not as the invited drivers had thought. Full results of that high-profile race are listed later (see page 51), but it proved too much for Dobbie as crowd figures were minimal and costs high.

Left: Future Indy Car Champion Danny Sullivan oversees the refuelling of his car during the 1975 Formula 3 meeting.

Below: Racing happened in all weather, with meteorological conditions often adding to the drama!

Chapter 1: The Tom Kinnaird Years

However, as reality set in, the money quickly ran out and Dobbie disappeared, leaving Tom Kinnaird with an improved, but sadly unfinished, motorsport centre. With the company in administration, Tom bought back the assets and chose to lease it out to a number of operators over the next ten years. With leases lasting only a year or two at a time, investment by leasees to improve the circuit was unlikely. No one was going to invest in capital expenditure when there was only a limited operating window in which to make a return.

During that time, the venue would function primarily aroud bike events with the Kirkcaldy and District Motorcycle Club, rallycross events, and occasional car race meetings run by the Lothian Car Club, Scottish Sporting Car Club and the RSAC. Knockhill would open in April and close after the final bike event of the season, usually at the beginning of October. In the mid-1980s this seasonal finale would become the showcase Jock Taylor Memorial Meeting, providing much-needed funds for while the circuit shut down for the winter.

Things would amble along, but occasionally high-profile riders such as Ron Haslam, Mick Grant and others would come north and all loved the challenging, undulating circuit. Dave Christie from Dunfermline was one of those who leased the track and Kirkcaldy motorcycle dealer Alan Duffus not only raced but also took a turn in leasing the venue to try and make a go of it. But, by June 1978, only four years after it opened, Kinnaird advertised Knockhill for sale. However, it remained unsold while the aforementioned leasees, and others, ran the circuit.

Top: Racers Dave Potter, Mick Grant and Jimmy Rae discuss tactics.

Bottom: A late 1970s photo of bike racers coming out of the hairpin. In those days, spectators were restricted to viewing from the Taylor's Turn hairpin to the first turn, and in the centre of the track only over the footbridge.

14   Knockhill: 50 Years of Racing

Right: Pictured here are Alister Lewis, Julia Bingham, Jimmy Law, Jock Taylor, Geroge Middleton, Benga Johansson and John Tawse in 1982. Jock Taylor had won the world championship in 1980.

Below: A montage of early car sport images by Iain Nicholson, all showing just how open and exposed the surrounding countryside was in the mid-1970s.

Chapter 1: The Tom Kinnaird Years 15

Left: Ian Nicholson's photo captures the barren surrounds of the circuit in the late 1970s and early 1980s.

Bottom left: An advert offering Knockhill Motor Racing Circuit for sale! It would take six years before a buyer was found.

Bottom right: Rallycross was thought to be a money-spinner for the operators; instead it proved a headache with all the humps and bumps, flooding and dust problems of a poorly constructed loose surface.

Opposite: Derek (right) has always been a high profile and popular figure within the racing paddock since the very first event and always around if a fellow competitor needed a helping hand.

That advert in June 1978 read:

For Sale by Private Treaty – Knockhill Motor Racing Circuit, together with ancillary buildings and equipment and 200 acres of valuable farmland.

Nobody was interested and the venue remained unsold for six years. That was until Kinnaird heard that the previously mentioned Derek Butcher, known to him through his appearances at bike race meetings, had recently sold his successful Fife Alarms business. Tom made an approach to Derek at the end of 1983 – and so the next chapter of the circuit was born. Derek took the plunge and bought Knockhill. This purchase marked the start of what would become Scotland's National Motorsport Centre.

Chapter 2
The Derek Butcher Era

Creating Scotland's National Motorsport Centre

Above and left: A montage of photos from Derek's personal collection of his very early days at Silloth, East Fortune and Knockhill.

Opposite: A Suzuki RG500 was one of several bikes that Derek raced in 1978 with much success, including setting the occasional lap record!

Originally hailing from Edinburgh, Derek Butcher moved to Fife to start his own alarm business. He became the second owner of Knockhill Racing Circuit at the end of 1983 and ran the business until he retired in February 2020. His influence, vision and dynamism forged the way forward throughout his tenure and has given us the Knockhill we know today. So let's hear Derek's story, in his own words, about how it all happened for the former owner and managing director of Knockhill.

Derek, you owned the track for thirty-seven years. Turning the clock back, what originally sparked your interest in bikes and cars?

Some friends first got me interested. I used to ride an ex-War Department motorcycle in the fields below the Pentland hills, probably illegal as I was only about fifteen years old. I had some fun on that 350 with three or four friends. Around that time, it was quite normal for people to commute to work on a motorbike. When I was seventeen, I had a 250 Ariel Arrow, using it for a while and then progressing up a 650 Triumph Bonneville, which was quite a sporty bike in its day.

A local man, Kenny Birch, used to pass by every weekend on his bike, which I think was a Norton Dominator, to see his girlfriend. He used to see me working on my bike, sitting on the pavement, cleaning it, polishing it and tinkering, and he said, "That's a nice bike, you should come racing." I said, "I don't know how to do that," and he said, "I do." So, he arranged to help me get my licence and he took me in his van down to Silloth Aerodrome in Northumberland when I was about twenty. I had a really exciting day of racing, camping on Saturday night, testing on Sunday morning, and three races on Sunday, in one of which I had a pretty spectacular crash. I was very lucky not to get hurt by the machines that were following me. When the day was over, I was hooked!

From that time what line of work were you in until you bought Knockhill?

I had qualified as an electrician and, when I was in my twenties, I moved to be an electrical engineer, fitting fire and burglar alarms, I did that for about three or four years and then when I was twenty-four or twenty-five I branched out on my own as I saw that there was no alarm company based in Fife at all. They were in Edinburgh, Glasgow or Dundee. So, working from home, I started Fife Alarm Services and after a slow couple of months it really took off, mainly through referrals and recommendations. So much so that after nine years I had sold about 2,200 alarm systems. Not on my own, of course! I had a team of about ten staff: two in administration and seven or eight installers and service engineers.

So what made you change? How did you hear that Knockhill was for sale and, ultimately, what made you buy it?

It was always for sale during the period of time I knew about it. It had been on sale continuously for about four years and, while it was up for sale, Tom Kinnaird, the owner, used to lease it out to various people such as Robbie Allen, Alan Duffus, Dave Christie and other people like that. What happened was that I got an offer, completely out of the blue, to sell my alarm business. It was a generous offer from a national company and I decided to take it. Tom Kinnaird had heard through the grapevine that I'd sold my business so he approached me and asked me if I'd be interested in taking on Knockhill. Of course, I was racing there at the time on bikes and was very much part of the scene, testing and racing perhaps ten times a year and I was only about thirty-one or thirty-two at the time, so decided to go for it.

Did you do any research or investigation about the business before signing on the dotted line? Or did you just go on gut feeling?

Basically, gut feeling, an inner drive that made me think I could make a go of it. The business has turned out completely differently and larger than I expected. I did think that I could do a good enough job with the initial business I was taking on. There were no books or records to view because the tenants Tom had rented it to didn't let him see their financial records, so he had nothing to base the last five years on, but I knew it was a good marketplace and a buoyant sport with good crowds, so I felt confident.

When you took Knockhill over, how long did you see yourself owning it? What was your vision for the years ahead at that time when you first took it over?

At that time it was just racing and testing and that was it, and private hires to companies. Business as we know it with vouchers, corporate days and other activities just did not exist, not even on the horizon; it was very much a racing business. I had a small team helping me, initially Maureen Jack in the office and Richard Crozier who had previously worked on the land when it was farmed. Richard left and a long-time ground staff team was formed of Geordie Melville, George Swanson and Alec Lees, with Stuart Gray starting his work here in about 1986. It has been great to have a team that stayed here for many years, with my daughter Jillian working from her teenage years, Laura Graham in sales, Ian Forrest on the operational side of things and Sandy Christie and Kenny Paterson as ground staff. We have essentially been building the business and building the venue simultaneously, bit by bit!

Did you have any early regrets or was it all about an attitude of heads down and keep going?

Well, it was a financial shock because my first year's turnover was £44,000 in sales and my second year was £90,000 in sales, but my spending was about £600,000, so the ratio of income to expenditure was catastrophic. It was because everything needed to be done, from electrical work, phone systems, toilet blocks, office areas, the medical centre, safety measures and a continual list of repairs and remedial works.

Opposite: Requiring assistance from marshals in front of a bumper crowd in 1978 at Knockhill.

Above: Setting a lap record at Beveridge Park in Kirkcaldy in 1980 on his Armstrong.

Chapter 2: The Derek Butcher Era

Top left: Always keen to drive anything with wheels! Driving a go-kart at the opening of the newly extended Knockhill.

Top right: Shell Oils were a keen early supporter and sponsor of Knockhill and Derek's efforts, and gifted him Knockhill's first permanently based ambulance. They were also one of the first to have their branding on the pedestrian footbridge over the circuit.

Bottom: Chatting with the starts – Derek talks with Donnie McLeod and Niall Mackenzie at a launch event.

Opposite, left: A turning point in the development of the business – the arrival of the AutoTrader British Touring Cars at the start of the 1990s.

Opposite, right: Investing in and training his team was all-important, for Derek, with the circuit being awarded Investors in People status. The accolade was presented by 1995 British Touring Car champion, John Cleland.

> " The track looked great when it was resurfaced, and it completely changed the look of Knockhill. Then when we got the white lines and the kerbs done it really looked terrific. "

What was your first event and how did it go?

It was April 1984 and we went for a bike meeting because historically a bike meeting always got good crowds, so we were hoping for 1,500 to 2,000, people, and the admission charge in those days was £2.50. Testing on Saturday was great, nice conditions, and bright, and everyone had a good time. Then on Saturday night, about four inches of snow fell. So, my first event was cancelled and I'd spent about £4,000 on advertising to try for a really big push to get a decent crowd of people to come to Knockhill. And all that money was lost. Which would have been about £20,000 nowadays, allowing for inflation.

What were your thoughts on the night of your first event when it was cancelled?

I was very disappointed, but I wasn't down because I knew we had other weekends coming up. What's lost is lost and you just have to keep going. Other people around and about me seemed to be far more devastated than I was. I just accepted it.

What was your driving force in the early years when so much money had to be spent on the venue and yet turnover was relatively modest?

I always felt there were bigger and better things to come for Knockhill. I felt the business I'd bought and had taken over was only like the first chapter. I was running it full time, being there six or seven days a week, and I had a team of people to help push it on, so I felt the circuit had a much better chance with me because previous tenants only opened it up on Friday, Saturday and Sunday.

Your first major investment was the resurfacing of the track in 1991 ahead of the Touring Cars coming in 1992. That must have been both exciting and nerve-wracking to make that huge outlay, as well as the fact that major British championships wanted to come north?

Yes, the track looked great when it was resurfaced, and it completely changed the look of Knockhill. Then when we got the white lines and the kerbs done it really looked terrific. It opened up the doors to attracting championships like Formula 3 single-seaters and it also kept the Touring Cars more attached to Knockhill because they could see we were investing in the future. Alan Gow of the BTCC was very supportive of us at the time because he knew we were continually investing.

Left: The introduction of Driving Experiences in the late 1980s marked a sea change in the operational activities on track. Four Ford Fiesta XR2s and six Formula Firsts were purchased from Brands Hatch Leisure.

Below: Future owner Derek Butcher competing on his 700cc Triton, taking Duffus Dip at speed at the opening event.

Opposite: Racing Formula Fords always appealed to Derek after his earlier passion for bikes. Their adjustability in set-ups attracted his engineering curiosity. He is seen here heading Sarah Playfair.

Personally, you've raced almost all your life. What have you raced and where have you raced?

I've raced at a couple of small tracks in Scotland up at Crimmond, Beveridge Park, Knockhill – of course! – East Fortune, Silloth, Crail and with cars I did Brands Hatch and I've been to Silverstone and Ingliston too.

Who did you enjoy watching from the early days of racing?

In the early days, people used to watch Alan Duffus because he always had good machinery and rode it spectacularly, so he was certainly someone I liked. I also really admired a small man from the West of Scotland called Bobby Steel, who rode a Rutherford Norton. He was a terrific rider and was a little tiger on a motorbike. He was amazing but, unfortunately, he was taken by cancer. He used to ride for Tom Rutherford from down in the Borders who built a McIntyre racing chassis and put a Commando 750 engine in it. I watched Bobby here and at Beveridge Park, plus he did the TT as well – an amazing rider and one I hugely admired.

What bikes have you raced, and which cars?

I've raced 125 Bultacos up to 250 Yamaha and 350 Yamaha, 500 RG Suzuki, 975cc Triumph Trident and in cars I've had a Caterham 7 – my first ever car – which I raced at Ingliston. In my very first race I was leading until the last corner of the last lap when I spun. I came in third after that!

So, you would have won the race if you hadn't crashed?

Exactly! That saying was made for me!

As a racer, have you always self-prepped your machines?

Oh yes, it's part of the sport, for me anyway. I like tinkering! The two strokes were pretty much sorted out by the Japanese and you didn't go too far away from their baseline settings, as they were so reliable. They were terrific but probably not as good a build as a British bike, but they steered, they braked and they were reliable.

It must have put you in a unique position to be a circuit owner and promoter, but also a competitor as well. I guess you could see it from both sides of the fence?

Yes, a lot of the competitors were friendly and quite open and would chat to me about what they saw as positives and perhaps point me in the direction of improvements. I think Knockhill had been very static in its condition for a lot of years and they could see that we were trying to improve it through hard graft, sweat and tears – and whatever money we were making we were putting back into the venue and everyone appreciated that, too.

Top left: The 25th anniversary was marked with a grand black-tie dinner at the Balmoral Hotel in Edinburgh.

Top right: Derek took every opportunity to race but this time he led the 25th anniversary parade on a bike school Honda Fireblade.

Right: At speed on his Ducati 1198.

Opposite: The Kawasaki 1000cc was a firm favourite too.

The circuit has improved dramatically over the years, but have you ever considered extending the track further?

Well, we looked at it and the expenditure to return doesn't really add up because it would be something of a slow burn. It would be a bit of a novelty I suppose to have a 2-mile track instead of a 1.3-mile track. After Clark's corner, turn right, go infield and do a big loop back out again. Halfway round Hislop's we had the Motor Sports Association – or it may have been called the RAC at that time – look at it, but the track inspector vetoed it because of the topography of the ground. Even though the existing Knockhill is full of rises, falls and undulations, what is here is here and that stays, but any new extension has got to be flat. That's because if you actually walk the ground infield, it drops away quite a bit as the return route would be on the rallycross track.

There have been vast improvements in the venue and some great events. Did you ever, at any time, consider admitting defeat and selling up or were you always happy to keep it going the whole time?

I am only human and, yes, there is only so much anyone can take! The worst was the first ten years, I would say. In terms of revenue, it was about ten years before you could say it was a proper business. Up to that point it was just one-way traffic financially. I was continually in the bank overdraft and it was really quite uncomfortable at times. It's never an easy business but, of course, it has a hugely enjoyable side to it which was what I was always working towards, as long as the money didn't run out completely!

> "Even though the existing Knockhill is full of rises, falls and undulations, what is here is here and that stays, but any new extension has got to be flat. That's because if you actually walk the ground infield, it drops away quite a bit as the return route would be on the rallycross track."

> **The life we have here is what I value, and if we ever forget that then it's never too long before we're reminded by visitors that it must be amazing to work here.**

During the last forty years what has been the most memorable bike you have ridden or road car or race car you have driven around here?

Memorable for being bad or good . . .

Both! I remember you raced a Formula Ford 2000 and Sierra Cosworth back in the day.

I loved my Reynard 2000, I did love that, and I also had a Toyota 1600 which was an ex-British Touring Car, an early model and it was terrific fun to drive. Bike-wise, the best bike I've ridden around here is an Armstrong 250, 2-stroke, Rotax engine but after that, when I was doing track days, I quite liked my Ducati. They were nice, rider-friendly bikes.

There have been some big highs but there have also been some sad times at the circuit. How did you deal with the lows?

The thing is that there are lows here but they are shared, discussed, talked about, re-enacted and spoken about, and it's a good thing that you're not in a solo situation. You don't always realise it, but actually sharing and talking about a cancelled event or rained off or winded off event – you know right away that you'll lose £20,000 for that weekend – but we all spoke about it and just planned for the future.

How proud are you that Knockhill Racing Circuit has stood the test of time and continues to deliver year after year?

Very, very proud and incredibly happy about it because a lot of people in the early years, and maybe some other circuit people who were around at the time, perhaps were a bit obstructive on our development and not very helpful; there were things like that, which was extremely disappointing. However, we just kept pushing on and did other things, did exhibitions and just basically left them in our wake, but it took five or six years for this to happen.

If you had a time machine, what would you do differently?

Do a business plan and take off the rose-tinted glasses! I could only see success by taking on Knockhill, I couldn't see anything else. It was going to be a success but it wasn't a sensible financial purchase and that was the thing. But I've had a great life here, so what do you value? The life we have here is what I value, and if we ever forget that then it's never too long before we're reminded by visitors that it must be amazing to work here. Actually, they're not far off – it is a fun place to work, too. No two days were ever the same. And, like they say, if you can find a job that doesn't feel like work then you're very lucky indeed.

And, finally, Knockhill has been such a huge part of your life. Can you sum up your thirty-seven years of owning Knockhill?

It's been a bit of an adventure, a working adventure! Every day was different, I've made some really great friends within the business and the sport, so I feel very lucky to have been involved in it for so many years.

Opposite: A return to his first love of bikes came after the introduction of the Clubman class with the newly formed KMSC Championship. A class that Derek would go on to win.

Right: The Butcher clan! Derek (back left) with youngest daughter Rosie, his elder daughter Jillian (centre) and in the front row sons Jamie and Rory in 1998.

Chapter 2: The Derek Butcher Era   29

Above: A Scottish motorsport dynasty! Rory Butcher (left) with his father Derek, sister Jillian and brother-in-law Gordon Shedden in 2017.

Opposite: Racing heritage. Jillian soon followed in her father's wheel-tracks, racing saloons and single seaters.

Chapter 3
Jillian Shedden

A Driving Force in a Changing World

Right: The eyes have it! Jillian gathering her thoughts just prior to a Formula Ford race at Silverstone.

Below: Always keen to be part of the team, Jillian is pictured with the Knockhill instructors – back row Sandy Forrest, Duncan Vincent, Graham Robertson and Titus Shaw; front row – Neil Hose and Barry Horne.

Opposite: A fast charging Jillian in her GBR Formula Ford Zetec leading Stuart Thorburn, Julian Taylor and Alan Brunton.

From the age of ten, Jillian Butcher (who would become Jillian Shedden in 2005) the eldest child of Derek Butcher, has had an influence and involvement in the development of Knockhill Racing Circuit. With her father's ownership from 1983, she was already far more interested in playing at Knockhill and becoming involved with numerous aspects of the business as a teenager, whether that was at the gate selling tickets and programmes or helping lap scoring in Race Control or in the Circuit Office.

Jillian became an integral part of the team running the circuit as soon as she left school and has had more influence than anyone in how Knockhill has become what it is today. Her involvement has been evident in every aspect of the business, the venue, its promotion, the activities and events that have become the mainstay of Knockhill. As well as being a highly experienced racer in her own right in saloons and single seaters, her knowledge and experience are recognised nationally by her peers and she has been on the Board of the Association of Circuit Owners, including a spell as its chair.

This is Jillian's story, in her own words:

With your dad owning Knockhill, what was your earliest memory? Was it like a big playground when you were a kid?

Yes, it certainly was. I would have been about seven or eight years old when he first bought Knockhill, so still quite young. In the very early years I wasn't allowed to come up here, but by the time I got to eleven or twelve it was a choice between going to Sunday school or Knockhill and you can guess which one I chose! In fact, I think there were three choices – Sunday school, ballet lessons and Knockhill, and I definitely chose Knockhill. It was very much a "one man and his dog" set-up back then and there were a lot of groundworks to be done, just general maintenance but from the ground up. Literally there was nothing here and Dad was out there putting fence posts in and building tyre walls and I would be sent off, initially just to the play park, but when I got older I was sent to the go-kart track on a go-kart, or to the car park on my motorbike, and I would have to go and find him again when I had run out of fuel.

It was that free. I was given so much freedom when I think about it now. A ten or eleven-year-old just going around the kart track with no adult supervision. But yes, I definitely had a helmet on! It was amazing really. Those were the very early years, but when I got a bit older I would start working to earn my pocket money.

Chapter 3: Jillian Shedden

When did you think you wanted to have a go at racing? When did that start?

That wasn't until much later on. When most people think about children going racing, they think they go karting aged eight, nine or ten and I really enjoyed driving a kart or riding on my off-road motorbike, but I didn't actually do the competitive side until I was actually driving on the roads. I think I was about eighteen or nineteen before I actually sat in a race car, so that was much later on.

Were you ever drawn to bikes for racing?

I was definitely drawn to bikes, bikes were my favourite sport, but it was hard enough getting my dad to agree for me to go in a race car. I'd had an off-road motorbike, but to go on the track wasn't really an option.

What was your first role working at Knockhill?

Selling programmes and tickets when I was young – probably twelve years old. Yes, I used to be in my little blue boilersuit and I had my bag of programmes and I would go up to each car as they came into the gate and offer them a programme for 50p! That was certainly quite a life experience. I was working with adults, and money, and I met a lot of interesting and colourful people.

You did timekeeping for the bikes from a very young age. What did that teach you?

Well, that was interesting because it wasn't like the computerised timekeeping we have now. You had to basically look out of the window and write down the number of the bikes as they passed; you had to consistently look out the window and not at the notepad! So yes, that was a really interesting time to be in Race Control as a young teenager and watch how a race meeting operated. Obviously, now I'm in Race Control and you've got all the technical equipment and backup to help. Back then you had people with stopwatches and people like me writing down the numbers. It was definitely a nice way to start learning how to run a race meeting.

What racers do you remember from when you were young, and who did you look up to at that time?

I remember the first time David Coulthard came to Knockhill and he was run by David Leslie Racing in a red Formula Ford and there was such a hoo-ha about him. He was definitely billed as the next big thing. He was obviously so young. He must have been seventeen, very young, and very much a rabbit-in-the-headlights guy. There were a lot of sponsors here and a lot of hype about him – and I think he went on to do great things!

Previous page: Jillian was fast in anything she raced – she's pictured here in a Zetec Formula Ford.

Opposite, top: Jillian raced nationally in the Zetec Ford Fiesta Championship supporting the British touring cars.

Opposite, bottom: Racing in the TOCA paddock in the Ford Credit Fiesta Championship resulted her being the leading lady racer and resulted in a prize drive in a Super Touring Mondeo.

Below: Going around the outside of someone at Duffus Dip is not for the faint-hearted but Jillian was a hard charger and battles it out with anyone side-by-side. Here she (33) duels with Simon Baker (31).

Left: Karting challenges were often end-of-season fun events with the Knockhill team taking on top racers in the paddock. Here Louis Di Resta (left) and Bryce Wilson (second left) finished first ahead of the Knockhill team of Graham Brunton, Stuart Gray, Alan Brunton, Mark Mitchell-Henry and Jillian Shedden.

Below: Jillian and Gordon Shedden share a love of motorsport in all its forms.

Opposite: Jillian says, "It was an honour to complete a pillion lap with my dad carrying the Commonwealth Torch ahead of the Glasgow Commonwealth Games in June 2014."

You took over the Knockhill helm at the end of February 2020 and then Covid-19 lockdowns started to strike in the middle of March. What was it like in those first few months?

Terrifying, to be honest. You feel like the world is coming to an end and no one knows what's going to happen. Initially, in the first four weeks, there was no indication of any government help, so yes, that was tricky. But what it did do was it really emphasised to me, or confirmed to me, that the team we've got and the commitment from the team we have here at Knockhill and the commitment they have to the business is exceptional. Everyone went through a bit of hardship during those times, but thankfully at Knockhill everyone's come out the other side. It was just really nice to come together as a team and know that we all worked to get through it. Although it wasn't good, there was definitely good that came out of it.

Reopening after each lockdown must have been challenging, but your customers must have equally been pleased to be returning?

You know what, opening up after lockdown was just the best feeling. But I would say one of the most gut-wrenching days we had here was when we ran the BTCC event behind closed doors. Thousands love the BTCC and I have been a fan of it since it first came in the early 1990s. It's always been the highlight of our year and you would get butterflies every time the event came to the venue. Then we were standing there with no crowd. It was actually one of the worst feelings in the world. So we were delivering the event, and it was on TV, but it was the worst event I have ever been at.

I was so happy to reopen the venue. Obviously, we had a few false starts like most businesses, but it was the most wonderful feeling; all the team were buzzing for it, all the customers were buzzing for it and it just made you feel that everything you'd put in, all the sleepless nights we'd had, were worthwhile, just to see the people back and enjoying themselves. It was really thrilling and made me proud, and the whole team felt really proud too.

People often ask if Knockhill will be extended. Do you see that happening at any time?

It's definitely something we have looked at and it's definitely something that would interest me because it would give more opportunities. From April to October we're fully booked at weekends, we can't fit any more in, and as you know we maximise each day including running at night and you really don't want to be turning people away. But we are almost at that stage of if you had a longer track, there's a possibility to have two tracks running at once. We are very limited with the space that we have and there would be a lot of compromises, then is it worth it? If you were to extend, for all the effort, would you actually achieve a lot more? We get a lot of good feedback about Knockhill, so my sense is if it isn't broke, don't fix it!

You hosted a royal visitor in May 2020 with Prince William, now Prince of Wales. What was it like meeting royalty, real royalty?

He was charming. He was as you would expect from someone you see in the public eye. He was just very sincere and very interested; obviously, off the back of Covid-19, we were just opening up or still on restricted operating and he was sincerely interested in how we had got on and coped during the Covid-19 times. Just an absolute dream guy really, he was lovely. I mean what a job he's got really. I think we were his third or fourth visit that day and he was going off to do more. He does do a lot for this country and he was everything you hoped for and more really.

Top: Jillian's husband Gordon is one of the most successful British drivers in recent times, winning three BTCC titles.

Bottom: Jillian's brother Rory is pushing hard to become a title challenger in the British Touring Cars, pictured here with BTCC pit lane interviewer Alan Hyde.

Opposite: Jillian pictured in June 2023 – driving Knockhill forward.

You have been investing heavily in technology with circuit-wide fibre optic cabling, FIA track safety lights and e-ticketing. What are your next investment plans for Knockhill?

With the technology that's always developing, we just need to make sure we're staying with it, so that's a challenge. We have a new hospitality suite which is called "The View at Knockhill", because one thing we have plenty of at Knockhill are the amazing views. Somebody walked into the reception a few months ago and said, "You've got the best view in Scotland," and I think he wasn't far wrong!

The View at Knockhill will be a nice addition to our armoury if you like; we're just really trying to make our facility better every year. A lot of work goes in over the winter as there's a lot of damage done in the bad weather with it being an outdoor venue – and it takes a long time for us to get back to square one. We have new karts, more cars, more hospitality and more of the same. We're doing the best we can and doing it better every year.

Your first season of ownership was 2020. How did it go and did you achieve every goal you set yourself?

To be honest, on paper, it may have been my first year in charge but I think I've been in charge for quite a long time before that! Yes, there were a lot of plans for that year and going forward as I believe there's so much more to come. But almost immediately Covid-19 struck and it was not until later in 2022 and this year that we could definitely bounce back after the lockdown interruptions.

What is your biggest challenge here on a daily basis?

The challenge is the variety – it's never the same and each day is different. I think sometimes that can be the challenge because you're maybe in the flow of working on something and then you've got something completely different to work on, whether that be the financial forecasting of the business or dealing with a drainage problem! That's how variable it can be and sometimes that can be distracting and you can't focus on the bigger picture. It's a challenge, but sometimes that's also the benefit.

Do you live Knockhill 24/7? If you do, how do you switch off at night, or do you just not switch off?

I do, obviously, have to switch off sometimes. My husband, Gordon, also works in the business and when you've got a partner working with you have to make a conscious effort to switch off. Sometimes I have to say, "stop talking to me about work," because I can't deal with it right now! You know, when you're standing there cooking the tea, or trying to watch rubbish on the TV. So you have to make a conscious effort, otherwise it may cause a problem. I do switch off and enjoy doing things that aren't motorsport related, although that's quite hard sometimes when your husband races. And your brother races. And I actually enjoy going to motorsport events as my hobby as well. But I like to go out on my mountain bike or road bike and do a bit of cycling or I do a bit of exercise at night to get away from it and get the frustration out in the gym. Yes, I definitely manage to switch off!

You have two family members racing head-to-head against each other in the BTCC. How was it watching your husband Gordon and your brother Rory racing against each other?

When we were watching in the garages, or wherever, and they were on TV, and the two of them would come close to each other, everyone would look at me – as if there's anything I can do about it! It's ridiculous really, as it's nothing to do with me, but it's an added dimension. It's stressful enough, but when there's the two of them together, it's just added stress and you hope that everyone keeps everything in perspective and remembers that it is only racing. It can be challenging!

What racing championships or series would you like to see at Knockhill?

I think we have the pinnacle of motorsport here with the BTCC and the BSB and I think we have to be realists as well that we're never going to get Formula 1. People who don't know much about motorsport always ask me if we can get a Scottish Formula 1 event and that's an absolute *NO*. I definitely think we have the best that this track can host in the BSB and BTCC events and we are doing a very good job of developing the programme. Family events are key, now including a new Truck Show this year. It's about history repeating itself as they were great family events in the early 1990s and they're coming back again. So, race series-wise, we have TCR-UK (Touring Car Racing) in 2023, which is a great up and coming championship, and it's brilliant that they have selected Knockhill for one of their events.

We're living in a challenging world regarding the use of fossil fuels. What mix of racing do you see in five or ten years' time?

I don't necessarily see a huge amount of electric racing. I know we have Formula E, but I don't think that will happen in club motorsport. I think the future for club motorsport is synthetic fuels. People will use their current race cars or race bikes but they will be using a fuel that isn't from a fossil source. That to me makes more sense. Even hydrogen makes more sense for us all – for us all to continue in our daily lives, not just racers. I have just bought my first electric car, but that isn't going to be for everyone – there's no way we can all be driving around in electric cars as there's just not the infrastructure and there isn't enough power in the country. So there's going to be a mix, and I think synthetic fuels are the answer for motorsport.

What's your proudest memory from being at Knockhill?

That's a really difficult one to answer – I think it was opening up again after Covid-19 and getting a crowd in. We were closed because everyone was furloughed, the venue hadn't been maintained and then you have a period of about four or five weeks to get everything opened up and ready again and to have a big crowd. The way we all pulled together was exceptional. When Covid-19 first hit it felt like it might be a bit of a break from work, which wouldn't be so bad, but it soon became clear how serious and deadly a situation it really was. We couldn't have known that it was going to become a two-year nightmare. Coming back to work after that worrying and stressful time was the best: it made me very happy.

PART TWO

Five Decades of Knockhill

Previous page: An impressive aerial view shows the full extent of the 220-acre venue of Knockhill

Above: Ian Forrest was a multiple race winner from the outset, winning at Ingliston and immediately after Knockhill opened. He would go on to become a long-time Knockhill employee and ultimately Circuit Manager.

Opposite: Oh I say! Rider Alastair King shows his appreciation of the champagne at the opening ceremony.

Chapter 4
The First Decade
The Challenging 1970s

We have already covered part of the story of Knockhill's first decade, from the early vision of Tom Kinnaird and David Brown to the ultimately over-ambitious plans of Denys Dobbie and his team. What was built was but a shadow of either party's dreams with the bare ribbon of tarmac laid on the side of a Fife hillside and a rallycross track threading its way through the middle. Buildings were few and far between, paddocks were grass, and safety – while advanced for the times compared to some other venues – none of these features were a patch on what they have become.

After the fanfare of two openings, the first with Geordie Buchan and Alastair King – pictured with Irene Sinclair, a tartan-skirted young woman from the Mid Argyll Motor Club – for the Kinnaird and Brown-led opening in September 1974, then the F5000 car opening in May 1975 under Dobbie's stewardship, there was much hype and anticipation for the future of motorsport in Scotland with this first, purpose-built facility. New Zealander Chris Amon, a star name from that era, was invited to do demo runs in his mighty F5000 Talon as part of the Lothian Car Club-organised event. Amon set a time of 54.1 seconds within the five-race format day which featured many local racers, some of whom would continue to race for several decades to come.

> "What was built was but a shadow of either party's dreams with the bare ribbon of tarmac laid on the side of a Fife hillside and a rallycross track threading its way through the middle."

Below: Sidecar action at the first event with building debris in the background and unfinished kerbs. But the riders loved the challenge of Scotland's newest track.

By August, a feature race was created with funding from BP, bringing twenty-four high-speed Formula 3 cars to the newly opened track. Patrick Neve, Danny Sullivan, Gunnar Nilsson, Rupert Keegan and Eddie Cheever were all aspiring young drivers who had sights on becoming Formula 1 or Indy Car drivers and a non-championship invitational race was created to try and attract the crowds. The BP Super Visco Static Formula 3 Race was held on 3 August, just over two months after Amon opened the Lothian Car Club event. All was not good on the financial side and the promised start and prize money did not materialise. Dobbie had to do deals with the gate money to make the race happen as some drivers were threatening not to race, to load their cars back on to their trailers, and head back down south again.

Above: Chris Amon interviewed after his F5000 drive in May 1975 with Denys Dobie to the left. Amon was presented a bottle of whisky by J. Dick Peddie, the Clerk of the Course, and interviewed by Jimmy McInnes.

Right: It was not plain sailing for the first car event in January 1975, with the event being abandoned due to mud!

Next page: Racing on the moon? Jim Dryden was a leading entrant in the mid-1970s. Here he drives up from the back straight, up the former loose section at the Tri-Oval, then turns right to a short straight that ran parallel to the current starting grid, before joining the tarmac surface at the brow of the main straight.

Chapter 4: The First Decade 47

50 Knockhill: 50 Years of Racing

BP Super Visco Static Formula 3 Race
Knockhill, 3 August 1975

1st Patrick Neve — Safir RJ03
2nd Danny Sullivan — Modus M1
3rd Gunnar Nilsson — March 753

Other notable entrants were:
5th Graham Hamilton — March 753
6th Pierre Dieudonne — March 753
7th Alex Ribeiro — March 753
8th Rupert Keegan — March 743

Local driver Andrew Jeffery (March 733 / Rtd)
and Eddie Cheever Modus M1 (Rtd)

Opposite, top: Saloon car action was strong in the 1970s. Duncan Fisher and Rod Birley are pictured here in 1975.

Opposite, bottom: Patrick Neve rounds Duffus Dip in the 1976 Indylantic race.

Below: The newly installed catch fencing required by the Motor Sports Association can clearly be seen behind, as Alex Ribeiro and Rupert Keegan round the hairpin.

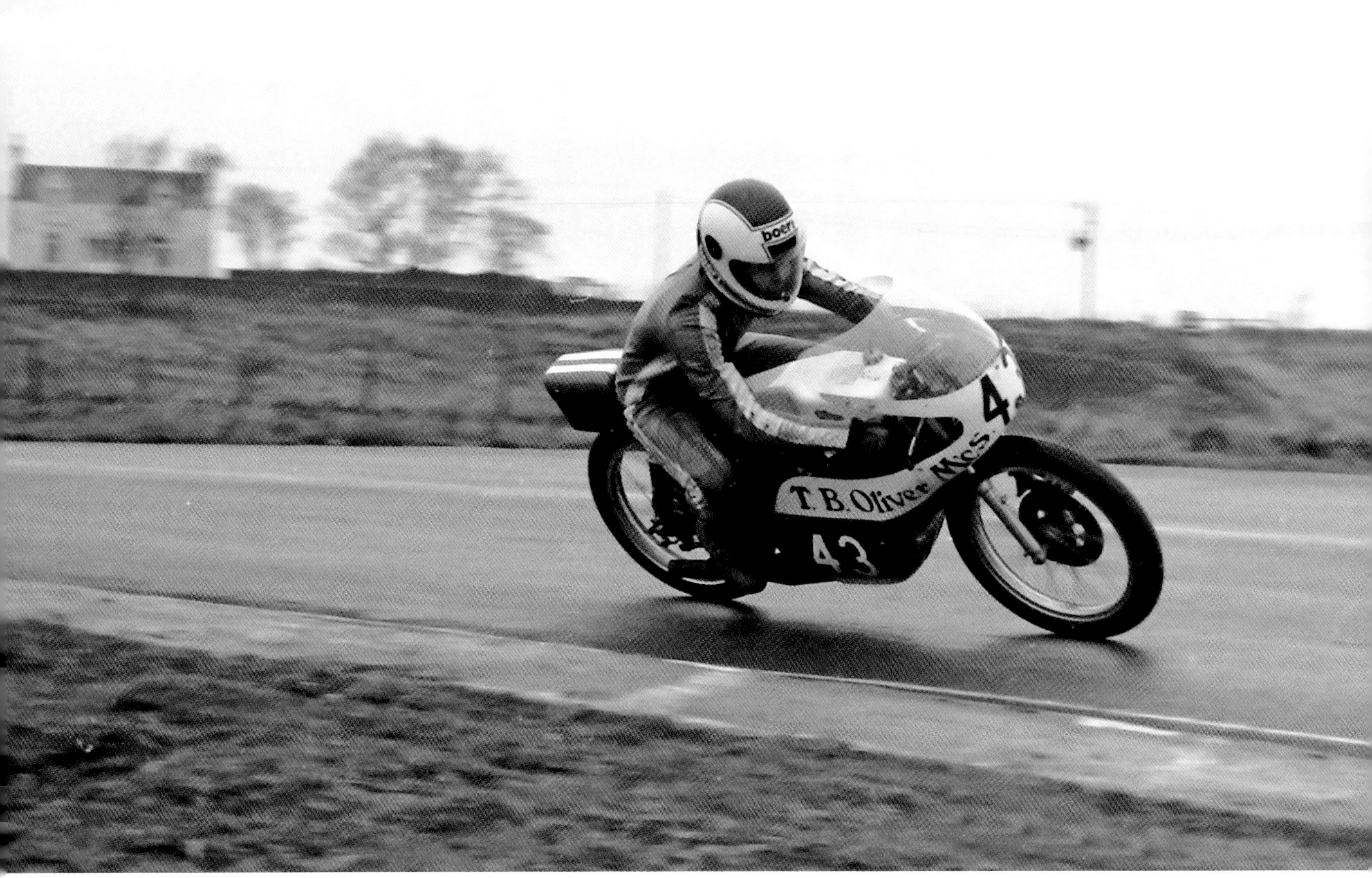

Above: Garry Hislop, brother of Steve, raced at Knockhill before he was tragically killed at Silloth, aged just nineteen.

Below: Closely packed mass starting grid formations are not allowed nowadays on safety grounds, but they were in the 1970s!

Opposite, top: By the late 1970s, the circuit operators had gradually extended the places that spectators could access to view races from. The first development was the final 300 metres on the hairpin approach.

Opposite, bottom: Fallen hero! Niall Mackenzie had his first ever crash at Knockhill, which was not of his own making as he was taken out. He is seen here (middle) sliding down Duffus Dip.

Phil Mellor (23) slips past a backmarker ahead of Scunthorpe's Adrian Marsh during some of the early 250 action.

...together now! Mick Grant (nearside) and Ron Haslam ...eelie their machines out of the tight Knockhill hairpin, ...ing the best crowd at the Fife circuit its money's worth.

HASLAM TURNS ON THE MAGIC

Knockhill road races by Andrew McKinnon

Pictures by Dan Jess

IT WAS the greatest thing to happen to Scottish motor cycle racing since the days of Bob McIntyre and Alastair King! The biggest crowd seen at Knockhill turned out to watch Ron Haslam perform pure magic.

Over 10,000 people braved gale force winds and driving rain to watch the best entry for a Scottish road race meeting. The Fife circuit, with a somewhat hazy view of the Forth Road Bridge on Sunday, was well and truly back on the map.

The truth is that the 1.1-mile hill top circuit was close to death's door. But a rescue party, led by the ever popular Haslam and comprising Mick Grant, Dave Potter, Graham Wood, Charlie Williams, Bernard Fau, Jacques Bolle and Michel Rastel gave the organisers a much needed shot in the arm.

Threatened with extinction, the demanding little track has been saved thanks to the VIP visitation.

The stars were seeded into two 1,000cc events and 250 and 350 specialists like Williams, Bolle, Phil Mellor, Neil Tuxworth, Graham Young and TT sensation Donnie Robinson got things off to a lively start in the smaller classes.

But it really was Haslam who stole the show with a spectacular wheelie demonstration out of the hairpin and over the brow of the hill on the start and finish straight.

... quite simply nobody north of the border had seen anything like it at Knockhill.

In the opening 1,000cc event he

look easy.

But then two laps from home Haslam went grass tracking at the Esses. The banking around the Esses is raised and in wall-of-death fashion the Langley Mill star hung onto the machine and got back into the race only to retire a lap later because there was so much mud on his 750 Yamaha!

So Fau went on for a win ahead of Wood, Bolle on his 250 Yamaha and Donnie McLeod and Adrian Marsh also on 250s.

For the other named riders there wasn't much luck. Mick Grant, who finished eighth in the opening race, never got above a midfield position and had to

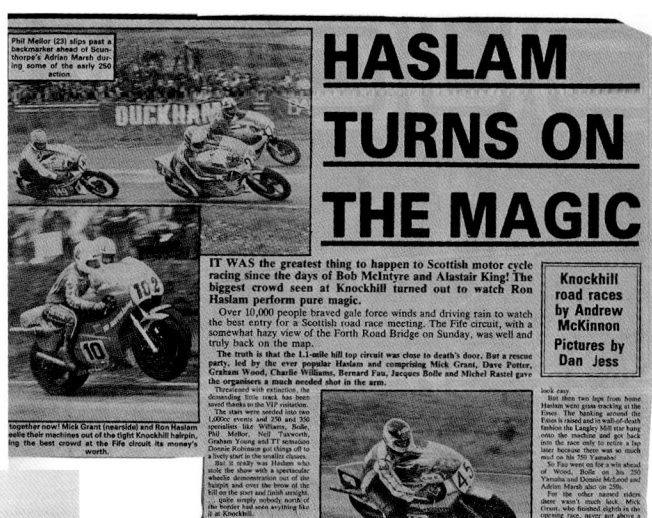

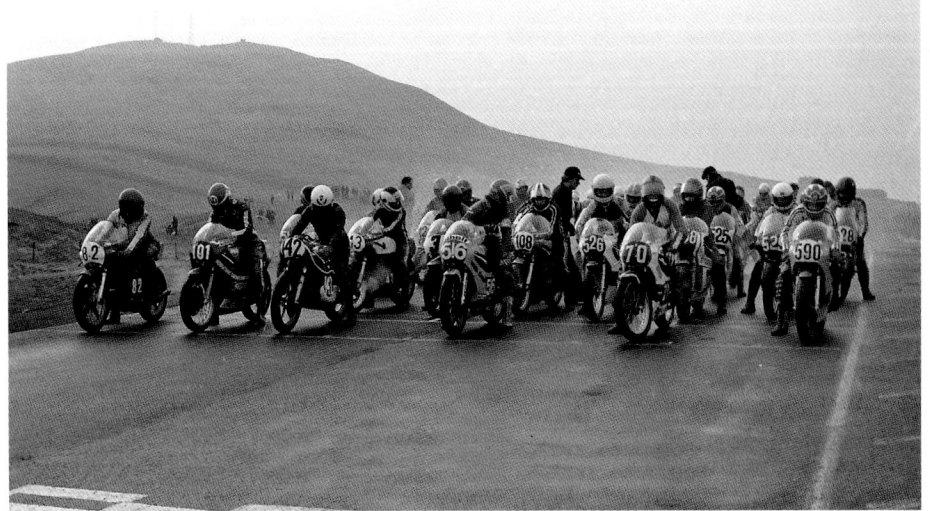

Chapter 4: The First Decade   53

Right: Circuit operator Alan Duffus in full "wheelie mode" exiting the hairpin at a time when photographers were allowed to stand at the apex of corners and within the tri-oval at the hairpin.

Below: Is this racing in Glen Coe? Sidecars in action, but the barren moorland of the venue can be clearly seen here with no trees in sight. A lot has changed over the years!

Opposite, top: The installation of the Bailey Bridge by Tom Kinnaird caused much debate with the planners of Fife Council owing to the temporary nature of its construction.

Opposite, bottom: One of photographer Dan Jess's favourite photos ever, as the legend Jock Taylor took time to smile for the camera as he flew past!

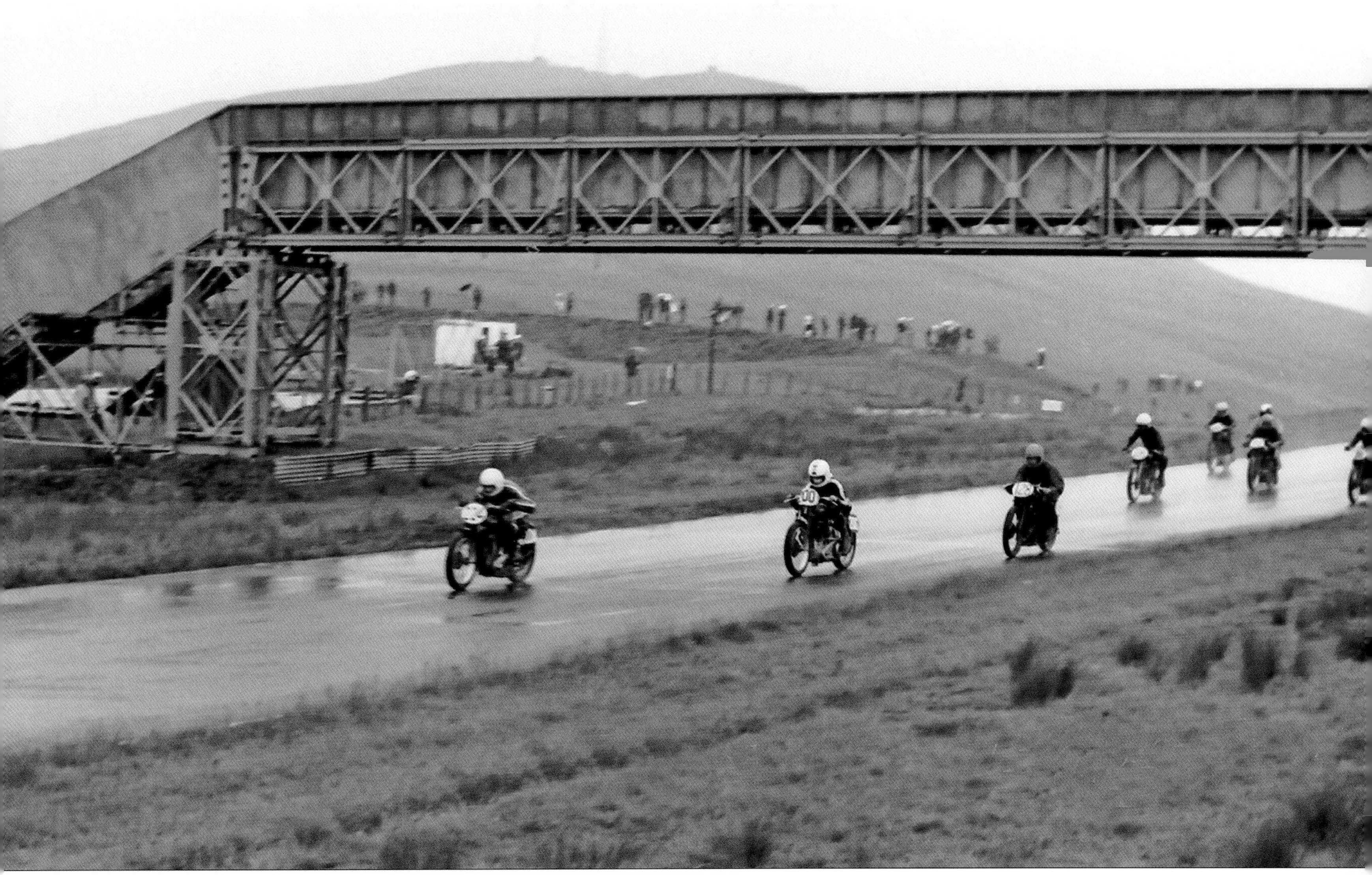

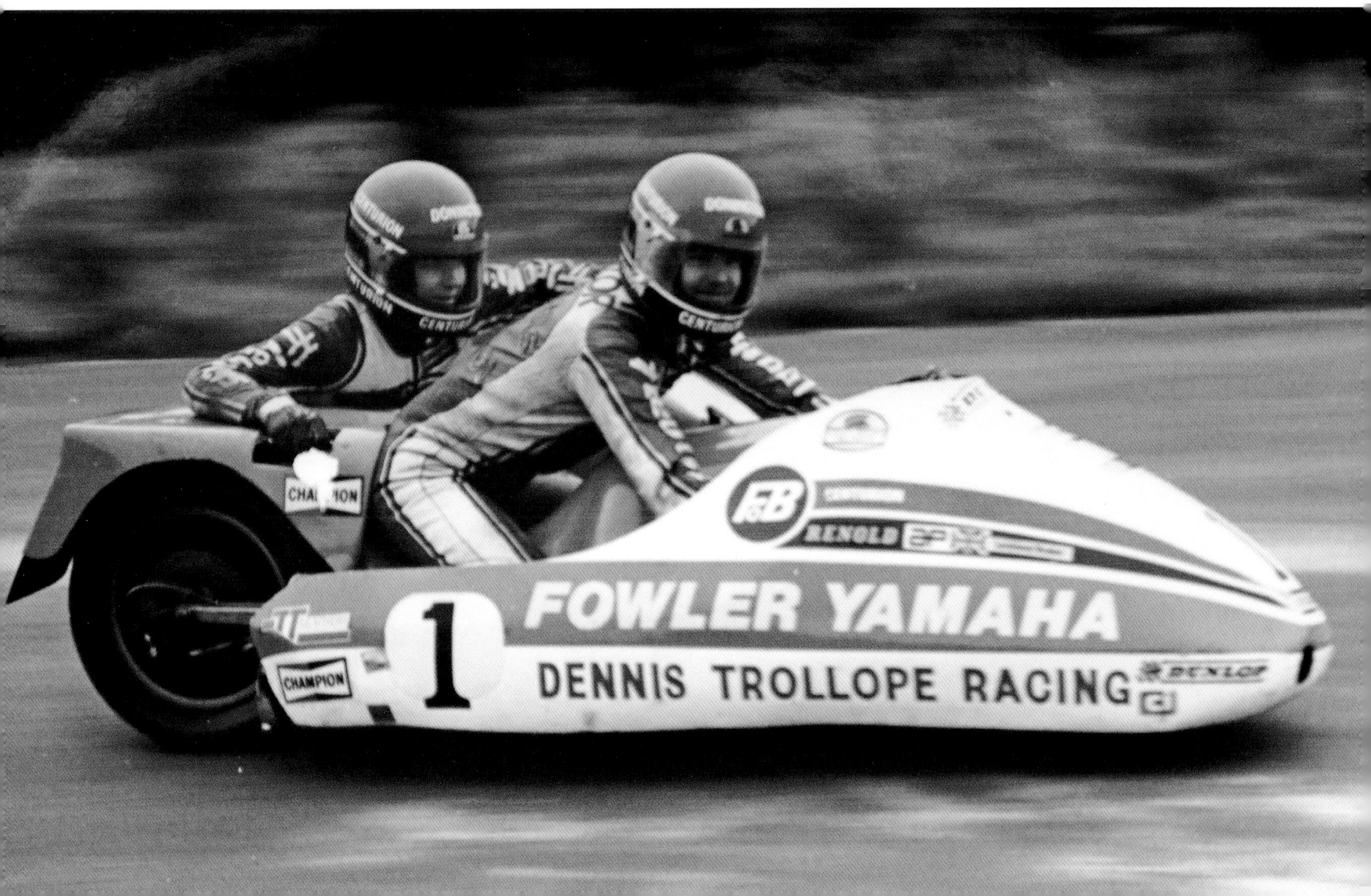
FOWLER YAMAHA
1
DENNIS TROLLOPE RACING
CHAMPION
CHAMPION
RENOLD
CENTURION
DUNLOP

Financial reality, the lack of crowds and weather-affected early events hit home and it was soon realised that the project was going to be a money pit. The dream soon turned into a nightmare, and Dobbie disappeared off the scene. This left Tom Kinnaird with no option but to buy back the assets of the operating company, after which he chose to lease the venue to a number of enthusiastic tenants, sometimes only on a yearly rolling basis. With no more appetite to invest in capital infrastructure and tenants unwilling to invest, the venue's facilities barely evolved in the first ten years. One of the biggest constructions was the pedestrian bridge, an ex-army Bailey bridge, to the infield which transformed early viewing options as the spectator areas did not reach beyond Duffus Dip, McIntyre's to the east, or beyond the Taylor's Turn hairpin to the west.

Above: A star in the making! David Leslie Jnr was a top National Kart racer in his early days before becoming a top single-seater, saloon car and GT sportscar racer. Here he rounds Clark's corner in his own inimitable style.

Right: It was soon realised that the configuration of Knockhill provided close racing for all types of racing events with the circuit's undulations adding to the challenges for club racers. Here a pack of saloon cars round the hairpin. Note the nature of the kerb, long grass and lack of spectator viewing area behind the track.

Chapter 4: The First Decade 57

Above: For car racers the flowing nature and speed of the circuit, when compared to Ingliston, provided a welcome mix between the two Scottish circuits.

Left: From Formula 3 single seaters to micro racing saloons, Knockhill welcomed an eclectic mix of racers, all eager to experience Britain's newest race circuit.

Opposite: After the mud bath that halted the first rallycross event, a large section of concrete was laid for the following season, much of which has now broken up and disappeared. A bespoke whin dust surface has now replaced the concrete that is almost dust-free for following competitors.

The SMRC ran car events exclusively at Ingliston, so any car race meetings at Knockhill were of non-Scottish Championship status run by clubs such as the Scottish Sporting Car Club, Lothian Car Club and the Royal Scottish Automobile Club. In this era, Formula Ford, Production Saloons, Modsports and GTs, Special Saloons and Formula Libre were the norm and saw leading drivers from Ingliston also race at the new Fife circuit. Ian Forrest, George Franchitti, Kenny Allen, John Fyda, Iain McLaren, Andrew Jeffery and Norman Dickson all featured at the early events, continuing their high-profile racing from earlier seasons across the Forth at Ingliston.

This meant that the mix of events began to focus primarily on bike events, which came to the fore after the closures of other airfield bike racing venues, and the once annually used Beveridge Park in Kirkcaldy. Knockhill's reputation as a bike track continued for some time with leading riders such as Bill Simpson, Jock Findlay, Bobby Steel, Stuart Cole, George Linder, John Stoddart (father of Suzie Wolff), Gordon Grigor, Derek Butcher and Jack Gow all showing their class at the KDMC-run events. These were interspersed with occasional rallycross and car events, as it was not until the late 1980s before SMRC ran a mix of events at both Ingliston and Knockhill, with Knockhill filling the void in the calendar when the Edinburgh venue reverted to the Highland Showground during June and July each year.

So, with the action primarily focused on bike sport during this early period, there were some top names travelling north such as the Dunlops, Mick Grant and a young Niall Mackenzie making his debut on a Yamaha RD350 LC. The finale to the season is what would become the Jock Taylor Memorial Meeting, which Knockhill funded star teams and riders to attend. At that time, club events would attract 500 to 1,000 spectators, but the well-funded October event would attract 3,000 to 4,000 because of the big names who were riding for start money and prize money.

One of the first events was rallycross, using the purpose-built undulating layout through the centre of the main track. It did not get off to a great start as the first club meeting had to be abandoned as the cars could not physically get from one end of the track to the other as the mud was so bad! As a result, the track was improved as there were prospects of hosting a British Championship round of the Lloyds & Scottish British Rallycross in the late 1970s, which would put Knockhill on the British motorsport map for the first time.

Opposite, top: The start of a racing dynasty – George Franchitti was a regular Formula Ford racer and winner!

Opposite, middle: Stuart Lawson was a highly competitive Formula Ford racer and would go on to become a Knockhill instructor when Knockhill started its own Racing Drivers school in the late 1980s.

Opposite, bottom: Dundee engine builder John Fyda (24) won a huge number of championships in Scotland and beyond in the Sports / Clubman categories.

Above: This is one of the earliest colour photos of Niall Mackenzie on his beloved Yamaha LC350 which he still owns to this day.

Next page: Le Mans starts were not uncommon, adding to the thrill and drama of Knockhill races. Crucial seconds could be gained, even before the turn of a wheel.

Chapter 4: The First Decade   63

Left: Gordon Grigor (117) raced at the earliest meeting in the 1970s and would go on to race successfully for five decades. Not only that, his son and grandson would race too..

Below: The first running of the Yamaha Pro-Am Championship featured the very best of young talent, all on identical Yamaha LC350s.

Opposite, top: State-of-the-art catch fencing was one of the Motor Sports Association requirements in order to obtain a track licence and host the 1975 Formula 3 feature race. The wooden posts and wire mesh fencing were designed to "catch" errant competitors, with the aim of doing so before they hit the armaco barriers behind.

Opposite, bottom: Push starts were the norm in the 1980s with the easy to start two-stroke engine bikes. Here Scott Fergusson (147), Stewart Cole and Roddy Taylor are ready for the off!

Rallycross was a big sport at the time, commanding primetime media weekend coverage from venues such as Lydden Hill, often commentated on by the late, great Murray Walker. With Lloyds & Scottish, which became Lloyds Bowmaker, the events at Knockhill were spectacular as they used the loose section through the middle of the venue, on to the back straight, then back on to the loose of the Tri-Oval (now tarmacked), then remaining on red shale as the track rose up the hill, parallel to the main race track, to rejoin the track at the start line. All in all, it provided the fastest rallycross track in Britain and was much liked by the drivers in their fast turbocharged four-wheel-drive supercars.

Such was the luck, or lack of it in this first decade, that the second Lothian Car Club event was reported by long-standing *Autosport* reporter and photographer Bill Henderson as having, "A poor entry for their seven-event BP Trophy Meeting, as well as having the weather conspire against them to deter spectators who also missed the dulcet tones of John Fife, since the PA equipment had been stolen overnight!"

This pattern of events remained fairly static for the first ten years, but things were about to change in September 1983 with the sale of the property to Fife businessman and bike racer Derek Butcher.

Chapter 4: The First Decade   65

Above: An unusual angle of early Formula Ford racing exiting Butcher's as they head up to the chicane. The dotted white circuit edge lines are shown, together with wire and catch fencing to the right.

Opposite, top: Early sports car racing round Embankment (Bend) before the Railway Straight which was the route of the old railway line from Saline. That line would help shape the layout of Knockhill.

Opposite, bottom: South Lethans farmhouse (behind) was used by the farmer before the circuit was established. It was not until the mid-1990s that it was purchased by the circuit.

Chapter 4: The First Decade

Left: The first rallycross track was beset with issues from the outset, if it was not flooding it had severe dust problems. Here its roughness can clearly be seen as it was also a "car breaker" and competitors were lucky to get to the end of an event without damage.

Chapter 4: The First Decade

Above: Kirkliston racer David Duffield was a highly successful racer backed by Caledon Coal, a company operated by Hugh McCaig, who was a huge supporter of Ingliston Circuit, Scotland's racing talent and Ecurie Ecosse. Hugh's interests were not confined to single seaters, but also included sports cars, BTCC and Le Mans.

Left: The Bailley Bridge dominates the horizon here which shows why it was challenged by the planners.

Opposite: Rally star Colin McRae was given a guest drive in the first British Touring Car event by ProDrive, as he had already become a household name in the rally scene.

Chapter 5
The Second Decade

The Start of the Derek Butcher Era

Above: One of the first big events hosted under Derek Butcher's ownership was the 1987 Formula 3 Scottish Superprix following teammate Damon Hill and Martin Donnelly. This re-enacted the high profile Formula 3 races some ten years earlier with the help of Danny Sullivan and Rupert Keegan. The first lap would not go well for Damon!

The start of Knockhill's second decade coincided almost perfectly with its purchase by Fife businessman Derek Butcher. At the time of his takeover in 1984, facilities were sparse, buildings consisted of Race Control, a bungalow as the Medical Centre, a café (half the size of the current Kinnaird's), and little else. And so began a long programme of investing in the circuit, the venue, activities and infrastructure to bring it up to the standards expected of what would become Scotland's National Motorsport Centre less than ten years later. Derek was not shy in investing in the business and one of his first acts was the purchase of one of the earliest fax machines in Scotland. The cost was £3,500 (£9,000 in today's money), and the joke was that seeing as how very few other people had one, who was going to fax Knockhill? But within a short while, it was in full use, sending and receiving faxes from all over the UK.

During the late 1980s, bike races were being run by the Kirkcaldy and District Motor Club as their main venue, Beveridge Park in Kirkcaldy, closed in 1988 after forty years. And there were very few car races, as the SMRC were solely running at Ingliston near Edinburgh. Car races at Knockhill were not Scottish Championship status and often had very small entries, given the pre-eminence of racing at Ingliston. Such was the low turnover and the seasonality of the business, Knockhill used to close over the winter but, from 1986 onwards, it was kept open all year round.

Midweek activities were often taken up by Tom Brown Racing School. At the time it was one of only a few places in the UK where a member of the public could drive a single-seat race car, in his case Van Diemens. Customers would be asked to use their own road car for the training element before experiencing the racing car. But then the Tom Brown Racing School had the opportunity to run at Ingliston Circuit and the request was made that they choose there, or Knockhill, and they chose Ingliston.

This resulted in Knockhill investing in their own Driving Experience fleet with the purchase of four Ford Fiesta XR2s and six ex-Brands Hatch Formula Firsts. Lead instructors were often the Knockhill management team with Ian Forrest and Stuart Gray hosting most of the days. This move to running their own driving experiences proved highly successful, as the cars could be used for both members of the public and corporate action days which were becoming increasingly popular. This was in the era before computers and the internet, and all purchases were via the post, so the office sales team would always look forward to seeing the postie in the run-up to Christmas. The larger his sack, the more sales were made that day! Add in thousands of calls per week and it was a very busy time in the office, but it all helped the cashflow in the winter!

Chapter 5: The Second Decade

There were no major sporting events other than the annual Shell-sponsored Scottish Super Prix in 1987 that attracted top Formula 3 racers such as Damon Hill and Martin Donnelly. This was much-hyped and had attracted both BBC Scotland and STV exposure before the event. The top teams had tested prior to the event with the Cellnet duo of Hill and Donnelly well ahead on the testing times. As the race started, the cars rushed down to the first corner and disaster struck for Hill as he went careering off, straight off into the backing at Duffus Dip having failed to negotiate the first corner – his race ending after only 400 metres. For two-wheeled racers, the Jock Taylor Memorial meeting was by far the most successful, as top riders and teams were offered start and prize money to come north, usually on the first weekend of October. With this end of season finale, and the growth of the Christmas voucher sales, these initiatives brought in very welcome income to keep the business open, and afloat, during the winter months.

The club bike scene was becoming stronger as sponsorship was landed from Regal Cigarettes in 1986. Not only did they contribute funds for prize money for the individual races, but they also provided blue Regal-branded huts, which became marshals' huts around the circuit, and sponsored one of the circuit's four Ford Fiesta XR2s used for the Driving Experiences. This sponsorship proved a valuable incentive for local racers such as Sandy Christie (whose father once ran the track as a leaseholder), Iain Simpson, Brian Morrison, Howard Selby, Roger Bennett, Eric MacFarlane, Ralph Boni, John Crawford, Jim Moodie and many others. The Regal 600s became the premier class with quality grids of around thirty riders. It was an impressive sight and sound, and really took the KDMC-run bike racing meets to a much higher level.

Above: The British Formula 3 racers spent days testing with the Cellnet team of Damon Hill and Martin Donnelly starting on the front row. This is a testing photo as Damon's race ended at the first corner after out-braking himself and slamming into the barriers at Duffus Dip.

Left: Penicuik rider Roger Bennett was a popular racer, not only in Scotland, but throughout the UK and beyond. His smooth, unruffled style was easy to spot and he was another rider who learned his craft at Knockhill.

Opposite: Tom Brown played an important part in the early days of Knockhill as he operated the Tom Brown Racing Drivers School – one of the first of its type in the UK. He would ultimately move his school to Ingliston, which opened the door for the Knockhill team to start their own racing drivers school.

Right: Sir Stirling Moss at speed during one of his three visits to Knockhill. He won the race, setting a lap record in a BMW Elva showing that he's still very much "got it" despite his age!

The Regal Championship also provided a great stepping stone for local riders, who could learn their race craft and pace on the tight, twisty and challenging circuit. Those who made that leap to the national scene included Steve Hislop, Jim Moodie, Ian Simpson and Iain Duffus, who would go on to star in both the short circuit and road racing scene. This peaked with a team of eight riders for the Celtic Match Races that would rotate between Scotland, Ireland, Wales and the Isle of Man, racing for the Celtic Sword. The Scottish team of 1988 was simply uncatchable; it was made up of a mix of riders who were competing nationally and internationally, and even included Steve Hislop, one of the greatest riders the world has ever seen.

To help try and appeal to a wider audience of car racing fans, in 1987 Sir Stirling Moss made the first of several visits north, and raced a BMW Elva owned by Allan Macgregor. His race win, which set a new lap record in the process, certainly was one of the higher profile wins of any car racer up to that point and helped raise the profile of Knockhill. Stirling Moss's appearance gained valuable column inches and photographs in the national press, but also attracted primetime TV news coverage. It was a real coup for Knockhill to have such a legend of motorsport lend his considerable influence and talents to the cause, and it showed what a gentleman and a brilliant driver Moss truly was.

Outwith the sporting events, two major public spectator events were hosted, firstly Off-Road Scotland that saw all manufacturers and dealers show off their latest 4x4s, and Supertruck Scotland. For both of these events, Knockhill was first and foremost the venue, and outside promotors (led by Gerry Maroney) would organise and advertise the events and take any profits, or losses! At Supertruck Scotland, top acts such as Steve Murty in his Jet Truck and the Pirelli Wheelie truck would woo the crowds, while the Scottish Tractor Pullers would create a lot of smoke and noise as they went for a "Full Pull!"

78 Knockhill: 50 Years of Racing

Opposite, top: Ouch! Drama at the hairpin. All race meetings relied on the help of countless marshals, here seen spinning to the aid of fallen riders.

Opposite, bottom: Donnie McLeod (243) leads Douglas Taylor (114) as they round McIntyre's. Note the total lack of protection for the spectators behind!

Above: Steve Webster and Tony Hewitt were sponsored by Knockhill Racing Circuit and carried the circuit's logo on their race machine for three seasons. A level of support that Steve still appreciates to this day.

Right: Launch of the Silverstone Armstrong race team featuring Niall Mackenzie and Donnie McLeod, who tackled the 250cc British and World Championships.

Investments came steadily off track with the building of Garages 1 to 10, with David Leslie Racing being the first tenant in Garage 4, running Allan McNish, David Coulthard and Dario Franchitti among others. All drove their first race car at Knockhill, often when not old enough to drive on the roads, but it served them well, being guided by two of the greatest contributors to Scottish, if not British, motorsport, in David Leslie Snr and David Leslie Jnr.

Once the ten garages were occupied, there was then a waiting list, so a further ten were built and occupied not long afterwards. By now, a twelve-year-old Jillian Butcher, daughter of Derek, was learning the ropes at Knockhill, working at the gate, in Race Control and helping where she could, all of which would help her in her major operational roles, not too much later.

In this period, Knockhill had a Suzuki bike school with Alan Eccles as chief instructor, using a fleet of Suzuki Gammas, something again that was ahead of its time. Two further bike schools would follow but the first was a taster of something that would become a major part of the circuit's revenue in the 2000s and beyond: the running of bike schools and track days.

For the most part, during the first ten years of ownership of Knockhill, the investments had all been off track with buildings, developing the business and activities, and the creation of the paddocks and then tarmacking them. Initially with lanes through the shale surface in Paddock 1, then tarmacking Paddock 1 with lanes in Paddock 2, before finally tarmacking Paddock 2 and creating a new paddock overlooking the circuit and the viewing banking. Such was the process of making profits, hopefully, then reinvesting in the business and the venue. It was a constant drive for revenue to develop Knockhill.

But in England, there were golden championships that would change the venue immeasurably: the AutoTrader British Touring Cars and the British Super Cup, which would become the British Superbikes. Initially, the touring cars would not come north as they ran a class structure, headed by the mighty Ford Sierra RS500s and their immense power. This was all to change for the 1992 season when the championship became too fast and expensive for the circuits down south, and the new two-litre category was created. This was Knockhill's chance to get into the big league by hosting a round of the BTCC. To allow this to happen, Derek Butcher's largest investment was needed for the first complete resurfacing of the circuit in November 1991. The investment needed to allow the BTCC to race on a perfect surface was £170,000, and along with some other necessary improvements, the spend was well over £200,000. A huge commitment, but the only way forward.

Top: In order to attract major events, large investments were required, with Tarmac Badstone restoring the circuit in November 1991.

Left: A great sight – Knockhill had not seen such quality car racing in its history until the BTCC arrived. The newly built assembly area was barely large enough to accommodate the show.

Opposite: David Leslie was a class act as he won in everything he raced. Here he leads in the Ecurie Ecosse Cavalier at the 1992 British Touring Car Championships. Note the size of the crowd! It was the largest ever seen at Knockhill.

Right: A star in the making. A young Dario Franchitti at the wheel of his Paul Stewart Racing Vauxhall Lotus, supporting the British Touring Cars.

Chapter 5: The Second Decade 81

Top: Always a crowd favourite, Sir Stirling Moss would spend as much time as he could mingling with fans and club racers alike.

Bottom: Binkie Chapman was a great asset to the Knockhill team in the early days with her exceptional admin role for Knockhill and the KMSC club. Binkie is pictured here with Andy Sim and Allan McNish.

During this period, Knockhill also hosted three rounds of the World Karting Championship with Martin Hines, Tim Parrott, Perry Grondstra and others between 1989 and 1992. Grondstra actually set the outright lap record of 50.1 seconds on his 250E kart, a record that would stand for years. With the specialist appeal of kart racing, initially the races would run on Sundays, but then an experiment to run on a Bank Holiday Monday did not prove a commercial success and was dropped.

In 1993, the finale of the season, the Jock Taylor Memorial Meeting, was one of the largest events that the circuit had hosted as the management team created the Scottish Superprix, an invitational race the likes of which Scottish race fans had never seen before. The star of the show was a returning Niall Mackenzie on his RoC Valvoline Yamaha Grand Prix bike. Rarely had a current world-class rider and his race bike been seen on a track in the UK, other than within the British Grand Prix event itself. Organisers paid start money to leading riders and put up a sizeable prize fund. The grid consisted of riders normally seen within the British Super Cup event hosted earlier in the year. James Whitham and Rob McElnea rode the Fast Orange Yamahas, Jim Moodie was on the Duckhams Norton and Steve Hislop rode the works Castrol Honda. What a race unfolded! The battle was titanic, with not an inch given or expected and there, at the front, was the duo of Mackenzie and local rider Sandy Christie. The two were side by side going through the chicane with Mackenzie winning by a wheel width from Christie with James Whitham third. An incredible race!

Top: Niall Mackenzie (11) and Gary Sanders competing at the end of season Jock Taylor event on 13 October 1985.

Middle: How things have changed! The grass paddock outside the marshals canteen near Kinnaird's Bistro, with everything a rider needs to stay on site!

Bottom: Roddy Taylor (106) was a highly successful racer on 125cc and 350cc Yamahas – here he is at speed as he rounds McIntyre's.

Chapter 5: The Second Decade   83

84 Knockhill: 50 Years of Racing

Opposite, top: Little and large: Knockhill has seen a huge variety of vehicles on its track over the years. This is an example of a large one; a Bentley Special being wrestled around the hairpin.

Opposite, bottom: Early visits by the touring cars immediately brought crowds the likes of which the venue has not seen before. A massive park and ride system had to be implemented using road closures and twenty-four double decker buses to cope with the crowd numbers.

Below: Two competitors at the top of their game. A young Steve Hislop is congratulated by five times British Rally Champion Jimmy McRae.

Next page, top left: In the late 1980s, there was a corrugated tin shed in the middle of Paddock 1, seen here behind the racers and their vehicles. Half was used as the scrutineering bay, half was used by the groundstaff team of Geordie Melville, young George Swanson and Alex Lees, before it was demolished to make way for the ever-increasing demands of the British touring cars for paddock space with their articulated lorries and awnings.

Next page, bottom left: Future Formula 1 stars Mika Hakkinen (10) in pole position with teammate Allan McNish (9) alongside in their Formula Vauxhall Lotus race cars, run by Dragon Motorsport, in May 1988.

Next page, top right: Cameron Binnie was a multiple Scottish champion in Formula Fords; his success at Ingliston and Knockhill was legendary.

Next page, bottom right: With the advent of the Hot Hatch Ford Fiesta and Golf GTI in the 1980s and early 1990s, saloon car racing saw boom times with the likes of Oly Ross taking the spoils.

The first AutoTrader British Touring Car event was very much a journey into the unknown and the crowd was modest, despite the nationally known names and Colin McRae making his race debut. Practice had gone well all week and star names such as John Cleland, Andy Rouse, Steve Soper, Tim Harvey, Jeff Allam, Patrick Watts, privateer Ian Forrest in his BMW M3 and many others graced the track in their BMWs, Toyotas, Mazdas and other marques.

Then, on race day, it rained and rained and then rained some more. John Cleland famously said, "I cannae see the track" while doing 130mph down the back straight. The back of the track looked like a battlefield with abandoned Vauxhall Junior cars everywhere and the event was a total washout. The Knockhill management team of Derek, Eric and Stuart gathered after the event and were lifted to a high when David Richards, the boss of ProDrive and a director of TOCA, sought the three out and said, "Don't worry, we will be back. You have a special circuit here and we must come back."

86   Knockhill: 50 Years of Racing

Chapter 5: The Second Decade 87

Around this time in the mid-1990s, the management team introduced track days for car and bike owners with the car versions becoming highly successful as they were turned into spectator events called Hot Hatch Days. These latched on to the "boy racer" market when Ford Fiestas, Vauxhall Novas and Astras, VW Golfs and Peugeot 205s were all the rage. Drivers would receive a briefing, and the circuit was controlled with traffic cones to help keep them on the racing line with drivers being grouped into sessions of twenty to twenty-five cars at a time for each ten-minute session. With strict policing and marshalling, these Hot Hatch days were certainly well attended with some exuberant driving styles making them highly entertaining. Thousands would come to the Hot Hatch Spectaculars that were created around the Max Power era of modifying cars, and show cars and trade stands would add to the festive feel.

With all the investment and the successes of hosting major events, Knockhill was granted the status of Scotland's National Motorsport Centre by the Royal Scottish Automobile Club; the RSAC was affiliated to the RAC in London, the then governing body of motorsport in the UK. This new status made for a fitting end to the first decade of Knockhill ownership by Derek Butcher.

Previous page: A young David Coulthard ready to exit the assembly area in his first full season of car racing in his Formula Ford in 1989.

Below: The straight between the chicane and Clark's corner is called Brabham's after a visit by Sir Jack Brabham. One of his sons, Gary, is seen here in his Formula 3 car.

Opposite: The 1990s saw Niall Mackenzie become the superstar he is after winning the British Superbike Championship in three consecutive years in 1996, 1997 and 1998. He would later describe this victory in 1998 as his hardest ever as he rounded teammate Steve Hislop on the last corner of the last lap.

Chapter 6
The Third Decade

Developing Scotland's National Motorsport Centre

And next, along came the Super Touring Cars! Vast manufacturer team budgets accompanied by equally large marketing budgets brought huge crowds to watch these cars in action. This explosion of cash saw many teams with millions of pounds at their disposal and drivers on six-figure salaries. Ex-Formula 1 competitors and Le Mans winners adorned the grid. To cope with the influx of spectators, up to twenty-four double-decker buses had to be hired, Park and Ride satellite facilities were provided and there were full road closures around the Knockhill circuit. This was truly a golden era, featuring drivers such as Gabriele Tarquini, Jason Plato, Alain Menu, Rickard Rydell, John Cleland, David Leslie, Steve Soper, Joachim "Smokin' Joe" Winkelhock, Frank Biela, Jan Lammers, Patrick Watts, Tim Harvey, Laurent Aiello, Yvan Muller, Will Hoy, James Thompson, Derek Warwick and many others.

Audi Sport was reputedly spending £10 million per season (£20 million at today's prices) running their two-car team. This was broken down as £5 million on the two cars and £5 million on hospitality and promotion. For each round, the hospitality unit would arrive ten days before the event and become a two-storey, glass-fronted structure with capacity for hundreds of guests. It was often said to be the best building ever constructed at Knockhill! Sadly, it had to be dismantled within three days of the event and moved to the next Touring Cars venue.

Opposite, top: The end-of-season Jock Taylor Trophy meeting was always a highlight of the bike racing season with riders attracted north with sizeable start and prize money available. Imperial Tobacco had sponsored the circuit and the Regal 600 Championship; the Knockhill Experience car doubled up as the winner's car with Jim Moodie, Niall Mackenzie and James Whitham on board.

Opposite, bottom: Dunfermline racer Sandy Christie was a class act when and wherever he raced, mainly on 600s and 1000cc bikes, including at the Isle of Man. His father, Dave Christie, was one of the lease holders who ran Knockhill during its challenging times in the late 1970s.

Below: Twice British Touring Car Champion John Cleland from the Borders was a huge favourite with fans at Knockhill. He certainly knew how to interact with his adoring supporters!

By 1994, Knockhill had become a regular fixture on the British Touring Cars calendar as the twisty, undulating terrain is unlike any other circuit in Great Britain. Cars leapt over the kerbs and seemed to literally fly around the short circuit, making it a firm fan favourite, and giving the TV cameras some spectacular and dramatic footage! In every respect, all the Scottish attention now centred on Knockhill, following the closure of Ingliston on safety grounds.

Chapter 6: The Third Decade

Right: The British Touring Cars have always been at the forefront of crowd entertainment. A young Matt Neal is perched on the windscreen while team members fire T-shirts into the crowd!

Below: The start of theSuper Touring era marked a huge change for the BTCC, with its stratospheric budgets and star drivers. The arrival of the Audi factory team in 1996 and 1997 ensured that the fans returned in massive numbers.

Top: At the height of the Super Touring BTCC era, every Touring Car driver, apart from the Scots, had Mc added to their name! This gesture was a witty act of appreciation, showing how much the teams loved coming to Scotland.

Left: Ex Formula 1 commentator Murray Walker was the voice of the AutoTrader British Touring Car era when it was on mainstream TV attracting millions of viewers. Murray is seen here chatting with Jennifer Birrell who was the BTCC co-ordinator and ran a tight ship when it came to standards of paddock layout and presentation which remain to this day with Dan Mayo in the role.

Above: For years, David Leslie was a leading driver in the BTCC, racing a Vauxhall, Nissan, Honda, Mazda and a Proton. He would be runner-up in the championship, but sadly he never won it outright.

Above: In 1999, the curcuit celebrated its 25th anniversary and invited back a whole host of bike racers who had achieved successes on the local, national and international stage. How many of these can you name?

❝ In 1999, Knockhill celebrated its 25th anniversary with a special bike meeting where a number of notable riders were invited to join in the celebrations with track parades on their original race bikes and some even racing within the event as well. ❞

Unfortunately, this level of manufacturer investment could not last. By the end of the decade, it had collapsed as these Formula 1-style budgets were not sustainable. The manufacturer-backed teams all pulled out and the championship reverted to being team-led. Many of those driving would be required to find their own budgets to allow them to race. The support classes at these events were also of considerable significance, giving aspiring young competitors the opportunity to race in front of large crowds. They also achieved the TV exposure that helped them pursue vitally necessary sponsorship. Among those succeeding in these endeavours and advancing to international success were Dario Franchitti, Ryan Dalziel and Kelvin Burt.

To accommodate the Touring Cars, the circuit went through some of its biggest changes. Banked spectator areas were created all the way around the track enabling a massive 23,000 people to attend the 1998 Scottish round of the BTCC. This event proved to be incredibly nerve-wracking for the whole team. The giant crowd was on site, but so too was low level cloud – at 300 metres above sea level, the other name for that is fog! The track action could not start until it lifted. As the minutes ticked by and turned to hours, tension mounted. Spectators, competitors, officials and, perhaps most of all, staff and management all looked anxiously to the skies. Derek's daughter Jillian, Knockhill's finance director, together with her organising team of Stuart, Gemma and Ian, had eyes and ears only for the weather conditions and a decision from Race Control. Would the day's meteorological conditions mean that the massive capital investment, hard work and commitment would result only in 23,000 refunds? When would it be safe for racing to start – if at all? At last, the weather cleared to reveal blue skies, at which point a revised timetable enabled some of the best Touring Car races of the entire season.

In 1999, Knockhill celebrated its 25th anniversary with a special bike meeting where a number of notable riders were invited to join in the celebrations with track parades on their original race bikes and some even racing within the event as well. In addition, on 11 June 1999 an anniversary dinner was held. This glittering occasion at the Balmoral Hotel in Edinburgh hosted a gathering of bike and car racing stars, many of them household names including John Cleland and Niall Mackenzie who were at the top of their game at that time, racers who had taken part in the very first bike and car events, and former operators of the venue such as Alan Duffus who had tried his hand at running the venue in those early challenging years. It was a spectacular night that also marked Derek's fifteen years at the helm.

One of the most spectacular and famous crashes in British Motorsport happened at Knockhill. Ex-Formula 1 driver Gabriele Tarquini was tipped into a multiple barrel roll by Tim Harvey, much to the amazement of the crowd. Standing at the corner was a teenager called Gordon Shedden with his father, and it was at this moment that he made his mind up to be a Touring Car driver! Many years later, Gabriele would return as a guest to Knockhill and said that his crash had created more worldwide publicity for Alfa Romeo than all their other racing that season.

Chapter 6: The Third Decade 99

However, with the celebrations over, the harsh reality of making ends meet for the business awaited. The stark realisation that Knockhill was still a seasonal business meant that new revenue sources had become necessary to bridge the cold financial gap of winter. Initially, contact was made with the Royal Highland Society with a view to running corporate group events at the old Ingliston circuit within the showground. Having considered various options, a new team was installed. Karts and quad bikes were purchased and 4x4s hired as required. And thus a subsidiary, Corporate Sport at Ingliston, was created.

The vision of Corporate Sport was to augment the year-round, end especially winter, activities at Knockhill. With its low-level location, only 20 minutes from the city centre and close to Edinburgh Airport with all the excellent road networks, the plan was that the new venture should be able to operate all year round. Sadly, the challenges of running live motorsport-related activities on an open site like the Royal Highland Showground proved problematic. Additionally, sales were hampered because corporate bookers wanted their guests to drive real racing cars on an actual race circuit and tended to see Ingliston as playing at being a "pretend racetrack". At the same time, karts, quad bikes and 4x4s just did not seem to cut the mustard and so the operating team and equipment was brought back to Knockhill after just two years.

Left: Marino Franchitti became the third member of the Franchitti family to race at Knockhill, following in the wheel tracks of his father George and brother Dario.

Below: The hosting of the PowerTour package finally brought more top level car racing to Knockhill with the British Formula 3 and GTs headlining. Anthony Davidson, Takumo Sato and James Courtney shared the Formula 3 podium with Sato finally breaking the long-standing outright lap record previously held by 250cc kart racer Perry Grondstra.

Next page: The British Superbikes have always attracted the largest crowds in Scotland with some 15,000 fans in attendance over the event weekend. Here Yukio Kagayama exits the hairpin in front of a mass of fans.

In 2001 a new concept in British car sport appeared, combining British Formula 3 and British GT in one package. And so, a top-quality national race series, Power Tour was born. It was designed to bring a family-led package of off-track entertainment with funfairs and other activities for the kids to make a "Day at the Races" more appealing for all the family. Its arrival in Knockhill was dramatic. Takuma Sato, who would go on to be a Formula 1 and Indy Car star, set a new outright lap record that would stand for years. In the GT element, Marino Franchitti's stunning car control came to the fore in heavy rains in the GT race as he produced a "Rainmeister" performance finishing a remarkable second overall in his GTO-class Porsche 911 GT3 RS, shared with Kelvin Burt, beating all but one of the more powerful GT-class cars.

Meanwhile, in 2000, a curious twist of opportunity arose when Circuit Manager, Ian Forrest, was on holiday in the Sierra Nevada mountains in Spain. One evening when Ian was relaxing in a cantina, the Knockhill logo on his shirt was spotted by one of the locals. This led to a conversation, in the course of which it emerged that this local man owned a motor racing facility nearby. Ian was taken to the Circuito de Guadix, not far from the city of Granada and its airport. The owner needed help managing the circuit and he asked if Ian and Knockhill could help. This sparked a new business opportunity and in 2001/2 Ian moved to Spain "on loan" from Knockhill, where he oversaw the running of the venue. Meanwhile, the team at home participated by sending race teams there for testing. The arrangement went sour as dealing with the Spanish temperament, business acumen and lacsidasical attitude to safe operational practices proved incompatible and it was decided to withdraw. Ian flew home and would continue as part of the Knockhill team for many years in the role as Circuit Manager.

Opposite: For the management team, diversification of the business has always been a driving force as it helps reduce the seasonality of income with motorsport events usually running from April to October. The building of Scotland's only publicly available Skid Pan and Driver Training Centre was designed to bring some welcome winter income. BTCC stars Anthony Reid and David Leslie are seen with the top brass from Fife Constabulary at its opening.

Below: Niall Mackenzie has been a loyal supporter of the circuit and the Knockhill Motor Sports Club riding a variety of race machinery. Here he is seen on his Virgin Yamaha BSB bike.

In the home motorcycle scene in the UK, and most notably in the British Superbike championship, there was a leaner period following the heady days of the Mackenzie era. Many Scottish riders had either retired from racing or moved on. This had a significant impact as the championship was weakened and the main grid was devoid of star names. In order to give the 2002 event a boost, the Knockhill events team approached Niall Mackenzie to ride one more time at the Scottish round of the BSB. Promoted as "The Return of the Mac", Niall was given a plum ride and works Suzuki GP World Champion Kevin Schwantz was the guest of honour. With a Suzuki promo, Kevin Schwantz demos, plus Niall Mackenzie and Schwantz on the bill, a healthy crowd was achieved at the joint biggest event of the year.

Left: The gradient changes are renowned around the world, which follow the topography of the land at Knockhill. This adds yet another challenge for man and machine, but provides fantastic viewing opportunities for spectators and eager photographers alike. Here Mark Wright (3), leads Sandy Christie (4), Roger Bennett (2) and Donald MacFadyen (1) in a round of the Regal 600 championship. This championship was highly funded and was once a guest race within a TOCA British Touring Car event, much to the amazement and awe of all watching.

Left: The PowerTour package of British Formula 3 and GTs were a regular visitor with Mario Franchetti putting in an astonishing drive in challenging conditions to win his class in 2001.

Below: Special feature bikes are often brought to Knockhill, here is Niall Mackenzie's own ROC Yamaha YZR500 GP bike.

Opposite: Two Grand Prix legends together. Texan Kevin Shwantz and Niall Mackenzie perform the opening ceremony for the new medical centre, flanked by Dr Neil Pryde (left) and circuit owner Derek Butcher.

As a venue, Knockhill was always improving with profits being ploughed back year on year. But no public funding was received and there were no external investors. Sadly, the medical centre was showing its age, becoming no longer fit for purpose. The next challenge was to work out how the circuit could build a new state-of-the-art facility that would become one of the best medical centres in the UK. The business of Knockhill Racing Ltd would gain no commercial benefit, but a modern medical centre was essential for sports purposes and the health and well-being of competitors. As such, because of the circumstances, it was possible to gain funding from the National Lottery as well as match-funding from public sources, and this combination of finances led to the provision of a superb new facility which was fit for purpose. The centre was opened by Niall Mackenzie and Kevin Schwantz during the 2002 Superbikes event under the proud and watchful eye of Knockhill's chief medical officer, Dr Neil Pryde, the driving force behind the project and his father, Joe, who was the architect. The drawings were subsequently donated to Brands Hatch so that an identical facility could be built there.

Elsewhere on the site, Knockhill was becoming more and more of a cluster for motorsport-related businesses who wanted to be based at the circuit. With a footfall of some 150,000-plus annually, it made perfect sense for businesses to be based in the hubbub of the main paddock which provided a perfect shop window for their services. Businesses have come and gone, but early adopters that remain to this day are Graham Brunton Racing, Scottish Legends Racing and WheelsAround. Graham has been coming to Knockhill since childhood, became a racer in Formula Ford and subsequently provided a race hire and preparation service, mainly relating to Formula Ford, and also supplying the Knockhill Ferrari and Aston Martin Experience on behalf of Knockhill. Scottish Legends Racing drove the introduction to Legends Racing within the SMRC racing scene and also provides a Legends Experience to members of the public. Ian Cowie Racing was among the first to offer a hire service for car racers, which has morphed into Paul Curtis Racing, which provides race hire and preparation services for Fiesta XR2 and STs owners.

To round off the third decade at Knockhill, one of the most spectacular events to occur at the venue did not happen on the race track! In the summer of 2003, Knockhill hosted Status Quo with 10,000 of their fans in Paddock 2, and the legendary band themselves supported by numerous local acts. It was a perfect summer's evening, without a breath of wind and the day-long music festival was topped off with a brilliant sunset as a backdrop to a spectacularly memorable night.

This diversity of activities with sporting events, vehicle and product launches, corporate days, press days, karting, music events and driving experiences gave rise to the company's slogan: "One Amazing Venue, So Many Uses". And this is still very much the mantra at Knockhill.

Left: Knockhill celebrated its 25th anniversary in 1999 and former operator Allan Duffus was on hand to chat about the early days.

Opposite: Attracting new events was a driving ambition of the management team, so as to bring alternative sports to Knockhill's regular and loyal spectators. The British Drifting Championships offered just such an opportunity with its rapid rise in popularity. The Knockhill layout started at the entry to Duffus Dip and finished at the exit of McIntyre's, offering one of the fastest drift tracks in the world.

Chapter 7
The Fourth Decade

Bringing New Events to Knockhill

Right: Three time British Touring Car Champion Gordon Shedden immediately became a home fan favourite, winning races multiple times – and he always celebrated in style.

Opposite, top: Another rising Scottish star was Jonny Adam, who dominated the SEAT Cupra Cup, winning it two years in a row, in 2007 and 2008, having previously won the Renault Clio Cup.

Opposite, bottom: Eurocars were brought to Knockhill for several years, featuring the Pick-Up Trucks, V6 and V8 Eurocars. These were the brainchild of engineering guru and short circuit racer Sonny Howard who loved the short twisty nature of Knockhill.

With the two major events of the British Superbikes and British Touring Car Championships visiting annually, the rest of the season was made up by SMRC race meetings and Scottish Championship bike meetings run by the KDMC. While the likes of Cleland, Reid and Leslie had dominated for over a decade, it was a host of young local Scots who would continue their legacy as they began to emerge from junior formulae. Two who were emerging fast were Gordon Shedden and Jonny Adam. Shedden was immediately successful in the Ford Credit Ford Fiesta Championship before moving on to the SEAT Cupra Championship and then landing a drive with Team Dynamics in the Honda backed set-up. Adam, meanwhile, joined the SEAT Cupra Championship, racing in it for multiple seasons and winning it in 2007, clinching the title at the Knockhill round. He did so with a stellar drive finishing some 20 seconds ahead of the runner-up, with one of his nine race wins that season. They would both join in the main BTCC championship later in the decade. Shedden would put his name in the history books with three championships, while Adam ultimately chose a GT sports car route and won the British GT championship multiple times. He was also twice a class winner at Le Mans, among numerous other sports car wins.

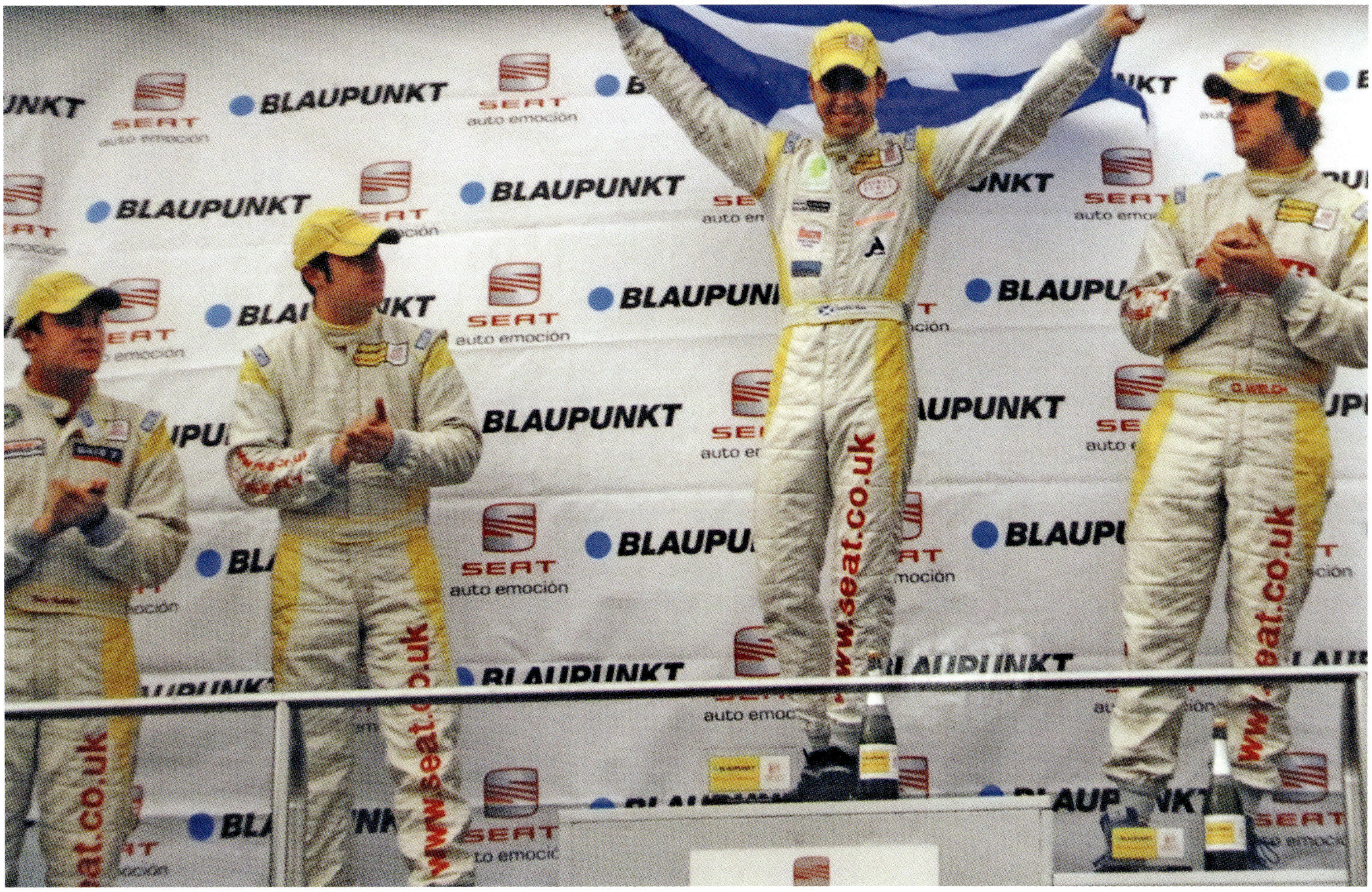
BLAUPUNKT
SEAT
auto emoción
www.seat.co.uk

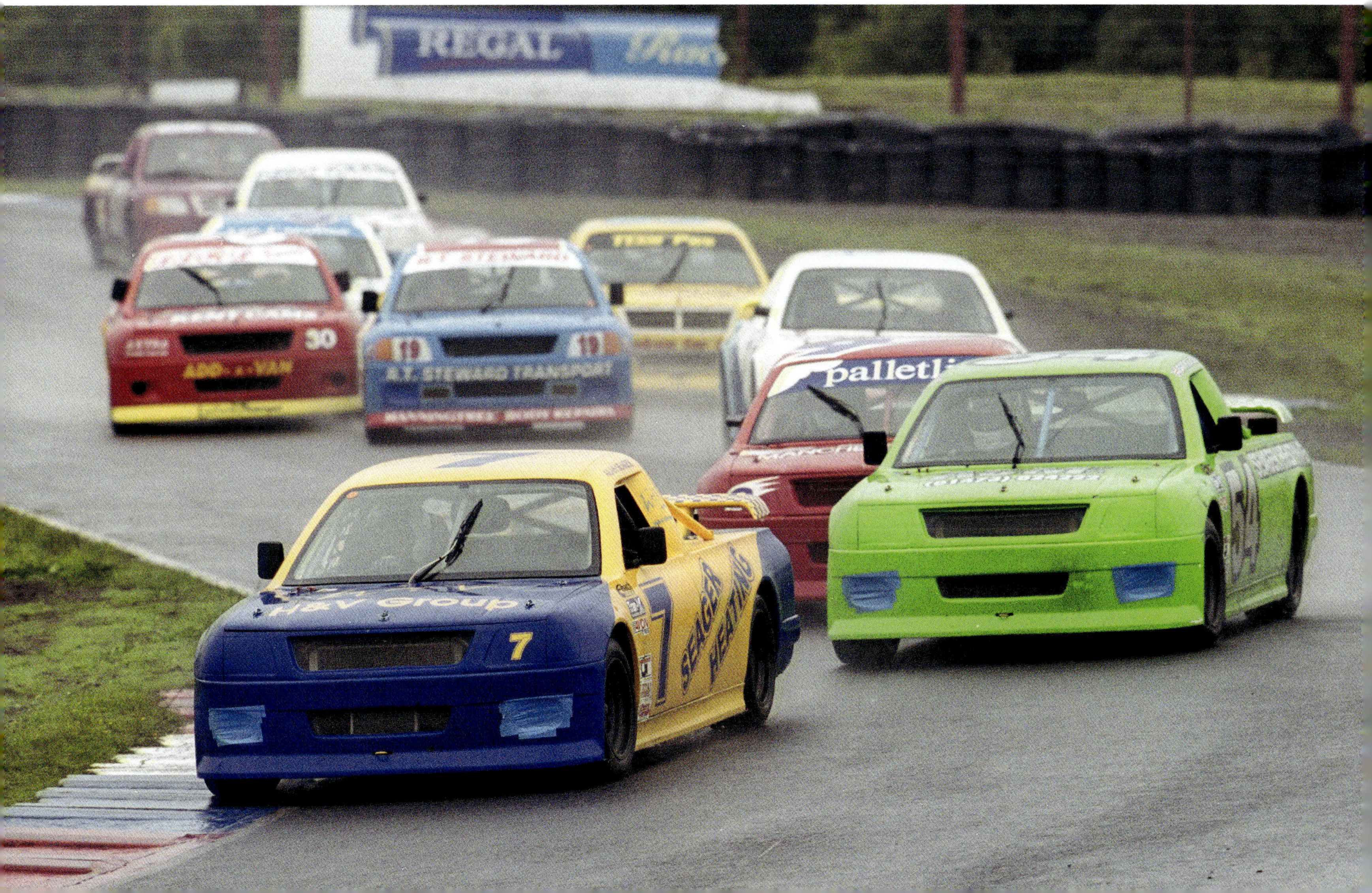
REGAL
R.T. STEWARD TRANSPORT
ADD-A-VAN
H&V Group
SEAGER HEATING
7

Tragedy struck in July 2003 with the death of TT and Superbike legend Steve Hislop in a helicopter crash. At the start of the 2004 season, with the blessing of the Hislop family, the originally named Railway Embankment, the section between Clark's corner and Taylor's Turn hairpin, was named Hislop's. Another air disaster befell BTCC and sportscar legend David Leslie who died a plane crash in March 2008, and such was his, and his father's, influence on Scottish motorsport, that the only left-hand corner on the track, at the bottom of Duffus Dip, was named Leslie's. From his own illustrious racing career to his fostering of young talent at Knockhill such as Allan McNish, Dario Franchitti and David Coulthard, among others, the Leslie name will forever be a part of Knockhill history. The memories of both Hislop and Leslie live on at their respective events as trophies are awarded in their names at the Superbikes and Touring Car events for the competitor that sets the fastest lap.

Top: Steve Hislop tragically lost his life after a helicopter accident in 2003. A tribute was hosted at the following BSB round with his bikes ridden by James Whitham, Stuart Easton and Niall Mackenzie. From that year onwards, the circuit awards the Steve Hislop Trophy to the rider who sets the fastest race lap every year.

Bottom: Working with Mission Motorsport and Disability Motorsport Scotland has been part of the Knockhill management's activities over the last ten years.

Opposite, top: Formula Ford had been a hugely popular training ground for future champions; the National Formula Ford is pictured here with a grid of almost thirty cars. Sadly, 2022 was to be the last year of a Scottish Formula Ford Championship for now.

Opposite, bottom: The SMRC introduced the concept of a one-make championship to Scotland with the Celtic Speed Minis proving to be one of the best and longest running.

Chapter 7: The Fourth Decade 115

Top: At the inaugural Scottish Classic SpeedFair, it was the only time in history that Sir Jackie Stewart shared the track with elder brother Jimmy Stewart.

Bottom: The GoFast Jet Pack man was a crowd pleaser, seen here "racing" a newly launched Ford Focus RS at the 2006 Motor Fair.

Opposite, top: Another highlight at the 2006 Motor Fair, a Ferrari Enzo FXX was driven by its owner Larry Kinch, one of only twenty-seven FXXs made by Ferrari.

Opposite, bottom: One of the all time top memories was made at the Scottish Motor Fair with Nathan Kinch driving an ex-Barrichello Ferrari Formula 1 car in 2006 – what a noise and what a speed!

By the mid to late 2000s, the Knockhill events team were setting their sights on organising their own major events, rather than solely relying on the ups and downs of championships travelling north. And so, two significant events were created, firstly the Scottish MotorFair and secondly, the Scottish Classic SpeedFair.

Following the demise of the Scottish Motor Show, which was the traditional format car show at the SECC in Glasgow, the team approached the Scottish Motor Trade Association and was granted rights to organise the Motor Show at Knockhill. This would be a reinvented show with live action, test drive options, celebrities, stunts and entertainment for all the family. The MotorFair highlight came when Aberdeen businessman Larry Kinch ran his 2006 ex-Schumacher/Barrichello Ferrari Formula 1 car, and his Ferrari Enzo FXX. The sights and sounds of those two cars on track will live on in the memories of all those who attended on that perfect summer's weekend.

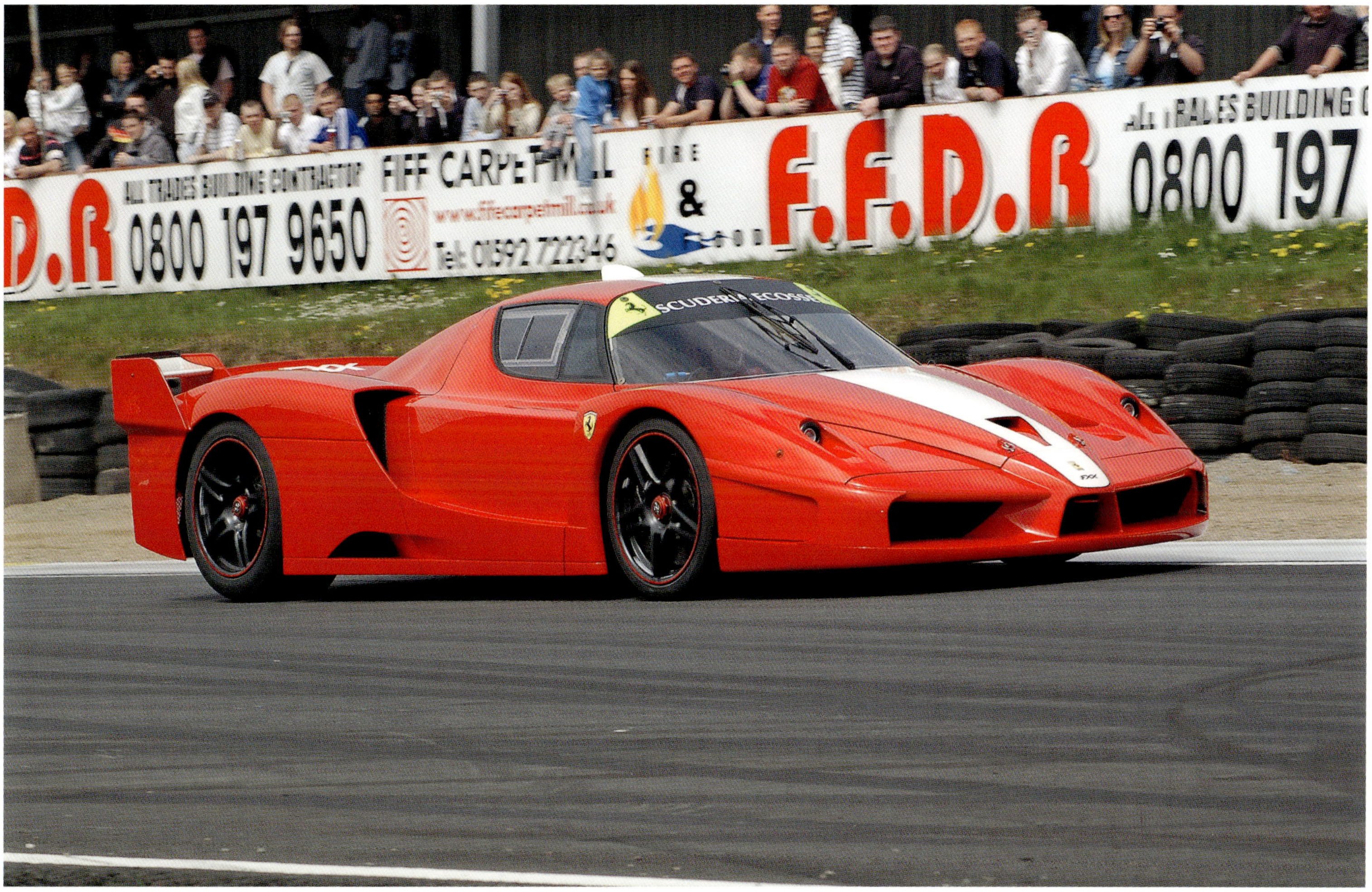

Chapter 7: The Fourth Decade   117

Classic SpeedFair was created in 2006 to mark fifty years of the SMRC and fifty years since Ecurie Ecosse won at Le Mans. With what promised to be the biggest classic-themed event hosted in Scotland, the Knockhill team got permission to close Princes Street, from the Mound to King's Stables Road, for a parade of Sir Jackie Stewart's Tyrrell, a Jim Clark Lotus, touring cars and Ecurie Ecosse Le Mans cars – all quite a sight for unsuspecting members of the public!

The first SpeedFair was a success and saw memorable moments such as the only time in history that Sir Jackie Stewart shared the same track, at the same time, with his older brother Jimmy, himself a racer in his earlier years until a crash curtailed his career. A large gathering of Ecurie Ecosse cars was on display on the track and elsewhere as a celebrated part of this splendid event. A Spitfire flew above, classic racing classes competed, while off track, an autotest and production car trial took place on the hillside, all brilliantly concluded with an open-topped bus taking the stars of fifty years of Scottish racing around the circuit.

In the second incarnation of SpeedFair, Sir Stirling Moss visited again and drove a recreation of a Vanwall on track. In the final SpeedFair event, the star guest was "Gentleman" Jack Sears, the first ever BTCC Champion and now president of the Ferrari Owners Club as they celebrated their own fifty-year anniversary. The Forth Road Bridge was commandeered for a promotional event as over one hundred Ferrari road cars gathered on the southside, to be paraded for the press, ahead of the weekend's event.

Above: Ron Cumming has been a regular at Knockhill since the earliest days in all sorts of sports and GT cars, winning multiple championships. His outings in a Footwork Formula 1 were a real crowd-pleaser.

Below: World stunt driver Terry Grant was a regular at all the car shows, entertaining the crowds on four and two wheels in his stunt cars and legends race car.

Opposite, top: Oops! Chaos during the Formula Junior race at the first Classic SpeedFair.

Opposite, bottom: One of the largest ever gatherings of Ecurie Ecosse cars was at the 2006 Classic SpeedFair, ranging from the 1956 Le Mans Jaguar to their British Touring Car. The iconic Ecurie Ecosse car transporter made the perfect backdrop.

Chapter 7: The Fourth Decade

"The Knockhill team got permission to close Princes Street, from the Mound to King's Stables Road, for a parade of Sir Jackie Stewart's Tyrrell, a Jim Clark Lotus, touring cars and Ecurie Ecosse Le Mans cars – all quite a sight for unsuspecting members of the public!"

Left: Before the 2006 Scottish SpeedFair, Knockhill was given permission to close the iconic Princes Street in Edinburgh with some of the historic race cars that would feature at this event. Here, Larry Kinch leads an awesome parade of Formula 1 cars including his ex-Jim Clark Lotus, behind is Sir Jackie Stewart's Tyrrell Formula 1, 1950s Ecurie Ecosse Jaguars, Ecurie Ecosse Le Mans C2s and the transporters of Ecurie Ecosse (left rear) and the Tyrrell Formula 1 team (right rear).

Chapter 7: The Fourth Decade

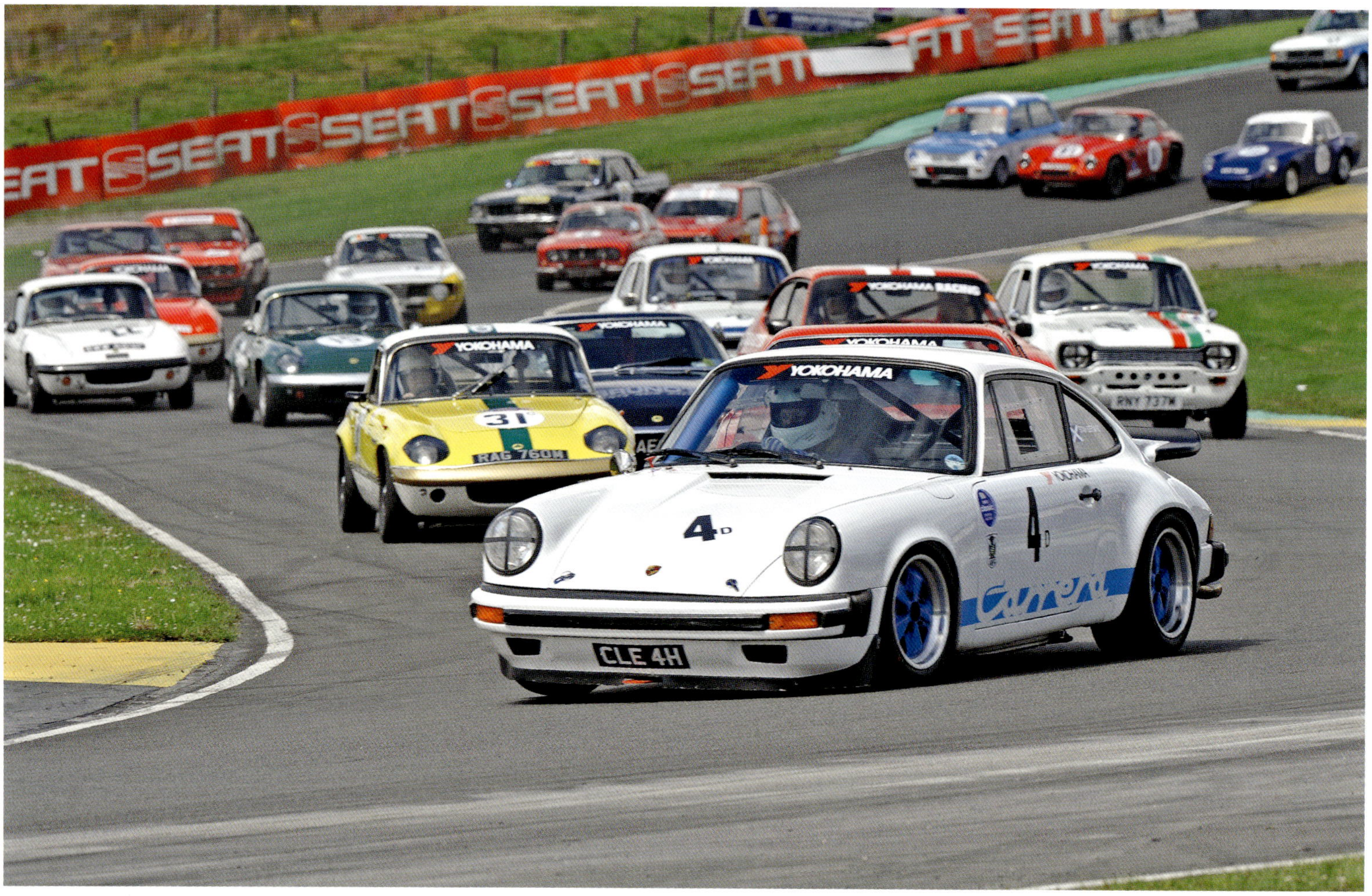
SEAT
YOKOHAMA
31
RAG 760H
4D
CLE 4H

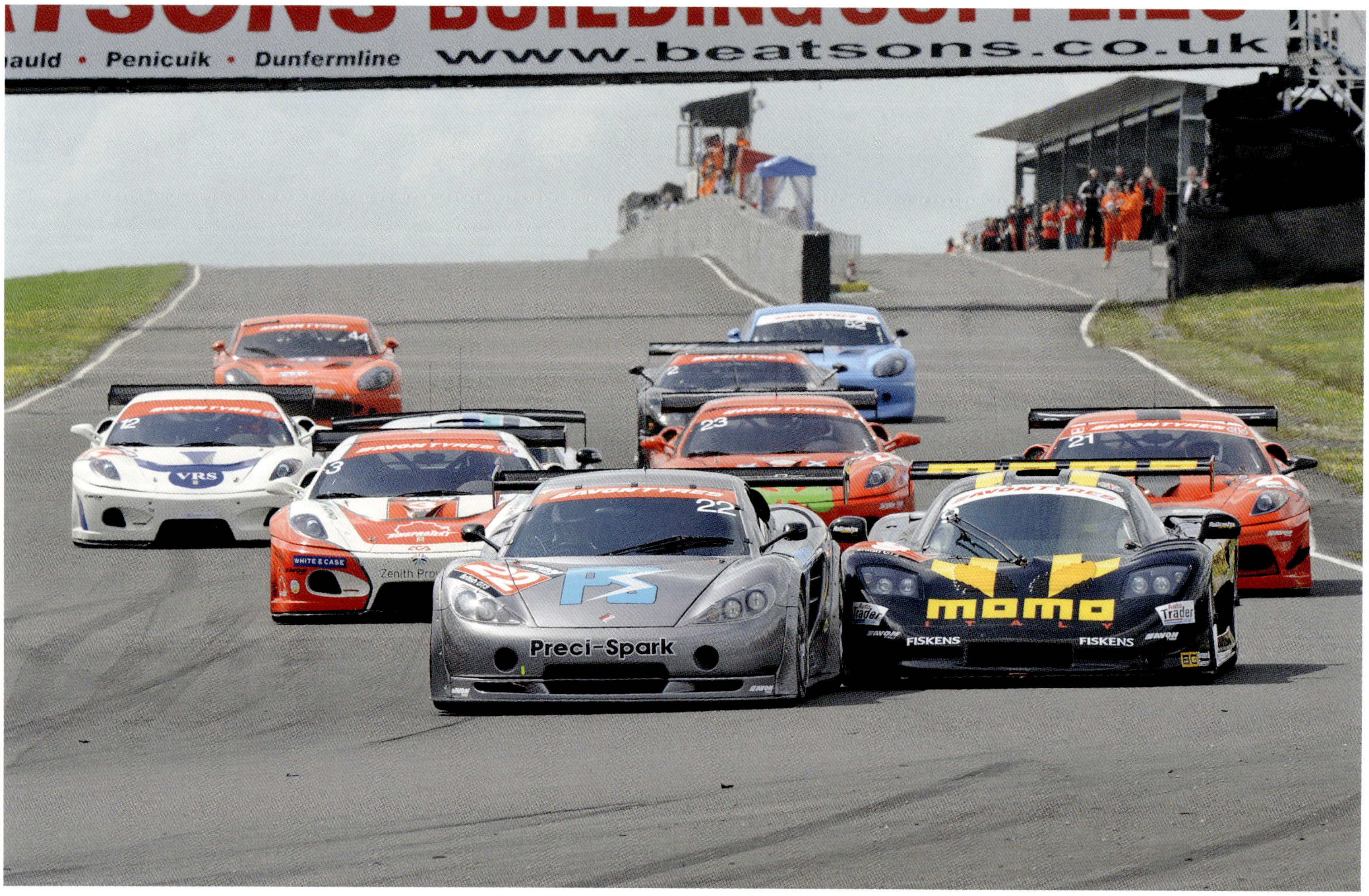
Penicuik • Dunfermline
www.beatsons.co.uk
Preci-Spark
momo
FISKENS
FISKENS

As the decade progressed, endless improvements to the venue were happening both trackside and off-track. On track, heightened safety regulations meant that crowd spectator areas were being pushed further back, gravel traps enlarged and debris fencing installed. One of the biggest changes for competitors, track day users, and Driving Experience customers, was the construction of the pit lane garages in 2009. Most garages at tracks are single or double to accommodate one or two cars per bay, but the decision was taken to build a single 50m x 10m open space with six double-sized doors. This was an inspired move as the large, versatile undercover space could be used in a multitude of ways.

Opposite, top: The SMRC-organised Scottish Classics have proved an enduring championships with big grids and an eclectic mix of iconic sports and saloon cars across the years.

Opposite, bottom: The Jones twins, David and Godfrey, dominated the PowerTour race on Sunday 9 May 2010 after winning both rounds at Knockhill that year while sharing their Ascari sports GT car.

Top: The mighty Audi Quattro Sport was brought to Knockhill for the SpeedFair event and was in pride of place outside the Circuit Office. It was also demoed on track, where it showed off its incredible power and unique sound.

Bottom: One of the largest capital investments was the construction of the pit lane garages in 2009, built by J&D Pierce.

But by 2009/10, the world had suffered a financial meltdown with a banking and credit recession and, as a direct result of this, the business mix at Knockhill changed dramatically. Previously, since the purchase of their own fleet of track cars for the gift voucher market, these same cars would be used midweek for corporate entertainment days, with groups of twenty to fifty per day. With the economic crash, this changed almost overnight and 25% of the turnover of the business disappeared. The Aberdeen oil sector had previously accounted for more than 50% of bookings and this dried up to almost zero.

Something had to change, and it was down to the management team to find ways to reinvent the business without major capital spends in a very challenging world. The circuit had been used previously in an anti-clockwise format, but this had not been popular after the death of a competitor leaving the short pit lane in the reverse direction, only to veer to the middle of the track and into oncoming riders. So, the team changed the pit lane exit and, without the option of pushing the run-off area at the hairpin head-on owing to the boundary of the venue, brought the track in by some twenty metres, thereby creating more run-off. For the previous thirty-five years, the track had been the same length, but this modification at the hairpin now shortened the track by some eight metres. Later, a land purchase was made to the west of the venue to allow a safety space beyond the hairpin, a new spectator area and a new access route behind the spectator banking. All of which was implemented as part of the continued improvements for visitors and to ensure the safety of competitors.

Below: Dennis Hobbs (25) was a front runner in the British Supersport Championship and would become a leading member of staff in the Knockhill team. Seen here following Stuart Easton in 2007.

Previous page: There can be no better sight in bike sport than a stunning grid of Superbikes rushing towards Duffus Dip after a race start. Here Stuart Easton, Shakey Byrne, Josh Brookes, Ryuichi Kiyonari, Michael Lafferty and others put on an amazing spectacle for the fans.

Above: The Ferrari Owners Club has hosted race meetings, gatherings and track days at Knockhill over the years, bringing a glamorous Italian spectacle to north Fife!

By 2010, the first priority was to make the most of every single event hosted at Knockhill and, sadly, the relationship between the KDMC bike club and Knockhill became strained. The KDMC chose not to continue running their meetings, so the Knockhill Motor Sports Club (KMSC) was formed with Niall Mackenzie as its president and Stuart Gray as its chairman. Its first season was 2011, and in 2012 the circuit was licensed again to run in both directions making it the only FIA-licensed international circuit able to run both clockwise and anti-clockwise, giving Scotland two full-time tracks at the one venue. This move was done, not only to provide variety for the track users, but it was also designed to reignite interest in the sport for competitors and fans alike, in light of the fact that the UK was experiencing a financial crash which had resulted in the almost complete loss of corporate days overnight. The management had to think fast as to how to replace this lost income and so the use of the track in both directions was investigated. This was not a new thing, as it had been used in both directions in its earliest years, but had fallen out of favour following a fatality. However, since modern safety standards were met, the track could be relicensed in both directions in time for the 2012 season.

At this time, Gordon Shedden's rise and dominance within the BTCC was relentless; he was already becoming a fan favourite before clinching his first title in the same year, 2012. This achievement – Shedden was the first Scottish champion since John Cleland in 1995 – with all his success and the endless media coverage it created brought the crowds back. Interest in the 2013 event was further heightened when Aiden Moffat debuted at Knockhill at the age of sixteen years and ten months, making him the youngest BTCC driver to date.

Right: Drifting originated in Japan, but one of the fastest and most challenging drifting tracks in the world is at Knockhill!

Below: Gordon "Flash" Shedden at the limit! Here Gordon flies through the chicane in the Honda Civic estate version of his BTCC car.

Chapter 7: The Fourth Decade

Top: Super Lap Scotland became an entry point for drivers wishing to make the step up from track days. Husband and wife duo of Adam and Fiona Kindness were key competitors from the outset. Here Adam blasts down the main straight in her trusty Subaru Impreza.

Bottom: Car owners of all makes and models are always keen to show off their cars. Here, the flags of these Hot Hatch owners show the country of origin of their car.

Opposite: Ashley Sutton has become a fans' favourite with his high-flying antics!

On the club scene, the Scottish Championship and KMSC events were immediately revamped into fast-moving formats and rider and spectator numbers rose. And in 2013, the first KMSC car event happened with the formation of Super Lap Scotland, a Super Sprint timed event to bridge the gap between track day driving and racing.

Throughout this decade, the management team faced a number of external economic challenges that were outwith their control and upon which they had to act quicky. Revenue streams that had been mainstays of the turnover changed to their detriment, almost overnight. Upon reflection, this ability to react positively to changing, challenging circumstances was achieved thanks to the small, independent nature of the ownership and management team of the company, which was able to respond deftly and open up new opportunities when others dried up.

Chapter 8
The Fifth Decade

A Changing and Challenging Era for Motorsport

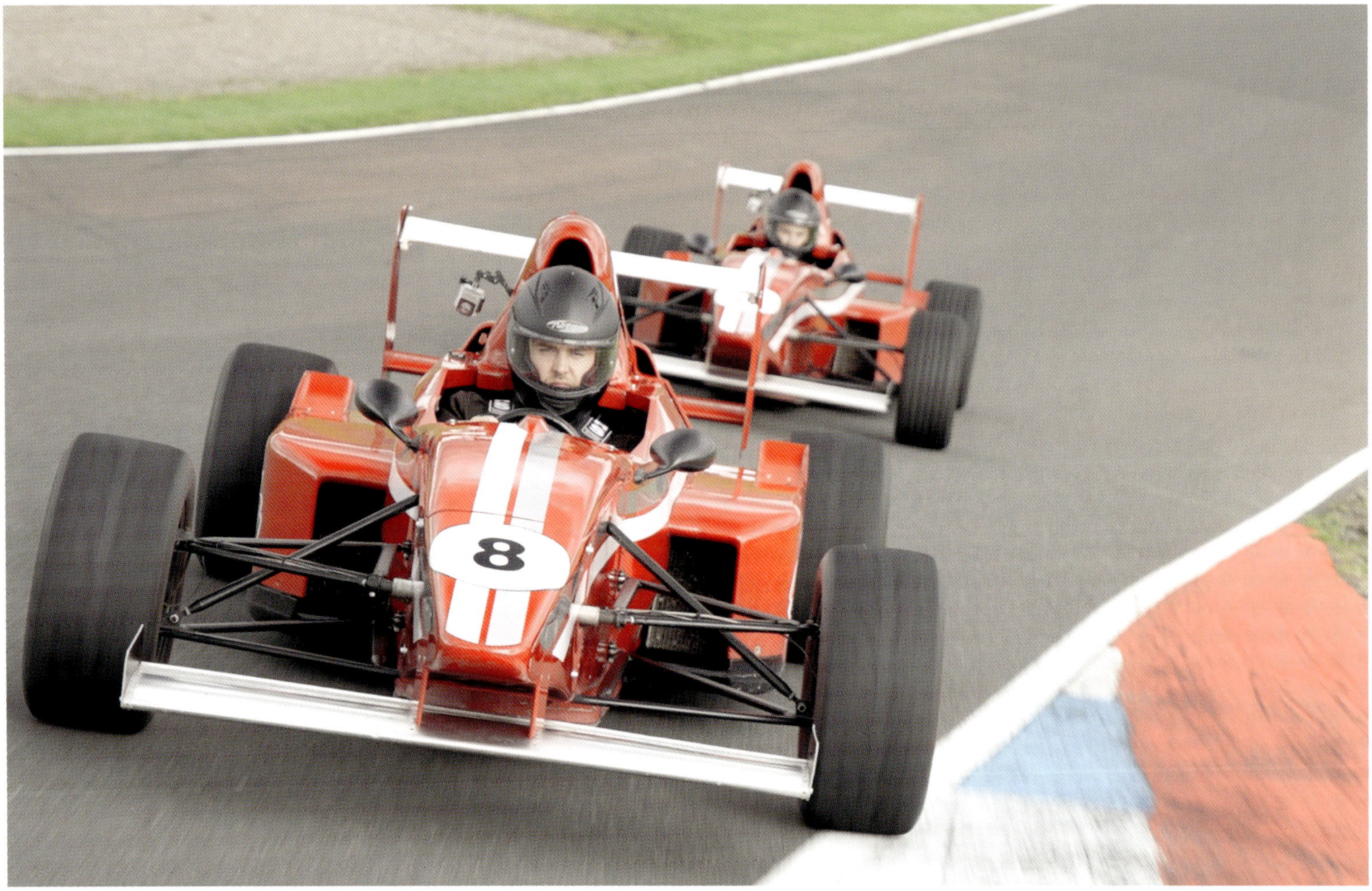
8

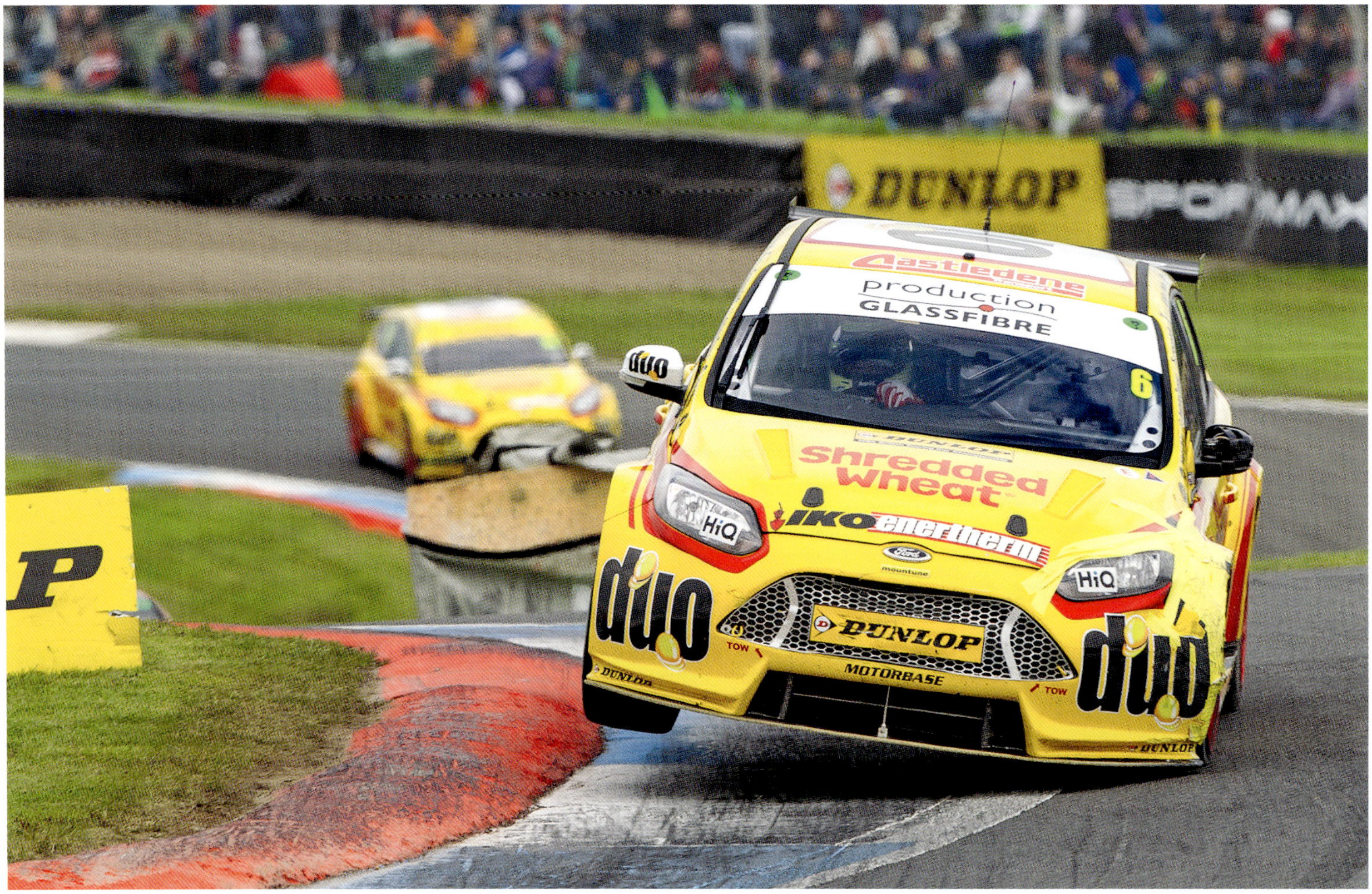
DUNLOP
production
GLASSFIBRE
Shredded
Wheat
duo
HiQ
DUNLOP
MOTORBASE

Local hero Gordon Shedden continued his starring role in BTCC with two further championship wins in front of crowds the likes of which had not been seen since the Super Touring era. His titles in 2015 and 2016 continued to encourage the strong interest in Touring Cars, especially as there were other competitive Scots in the grid including Aiden Moffat, with Dave Newsham, Glynn Geddie, Derek Palmer Jnr, Kieran Gallagher and others all joining during the next decade. It was, however, in August 2017 that Gordon's brother-in-law Rory Butcher, Jillian's brother, joined the BTCC grid. Rory had been a successful Formula Ford and GT racer to a high level and a career switch opportunity arose in 2017 to join Motorbase mid-season in the Shredded Wheat-backed Ford Focus. This move created the unusual spectacle of family members duelling wheel to wheel, both in front-running cars. With Gordon loyal to Honda and Rory racing a mixture of a Ford, MG, Honda and Toyota, the two brothers-in-law would fly the flag for Scotland across the UK.

Opposite, top: A fleet of Audi-engined Formula race cars was purchased to replace the original Formula Firsts and proved an immediate hit for the Driving Experience customers. These are used by both members of the public who have a gift voucher as well as mid-week corporate groups.

Opposite, bottom: Rory Butcher made his BTCC debut in August 2017 and was immediately on the pace. The Kirkcaldy-based driver, and son of owner Derek, is a fan favourite with his flamboyant style.

Below: One of the biggest successes has been the return of SuperTruck Scotland organised by the Knockhill Events Team and is hoped it will be a winner for years to come.

Chapter 8: The Fifth Decade

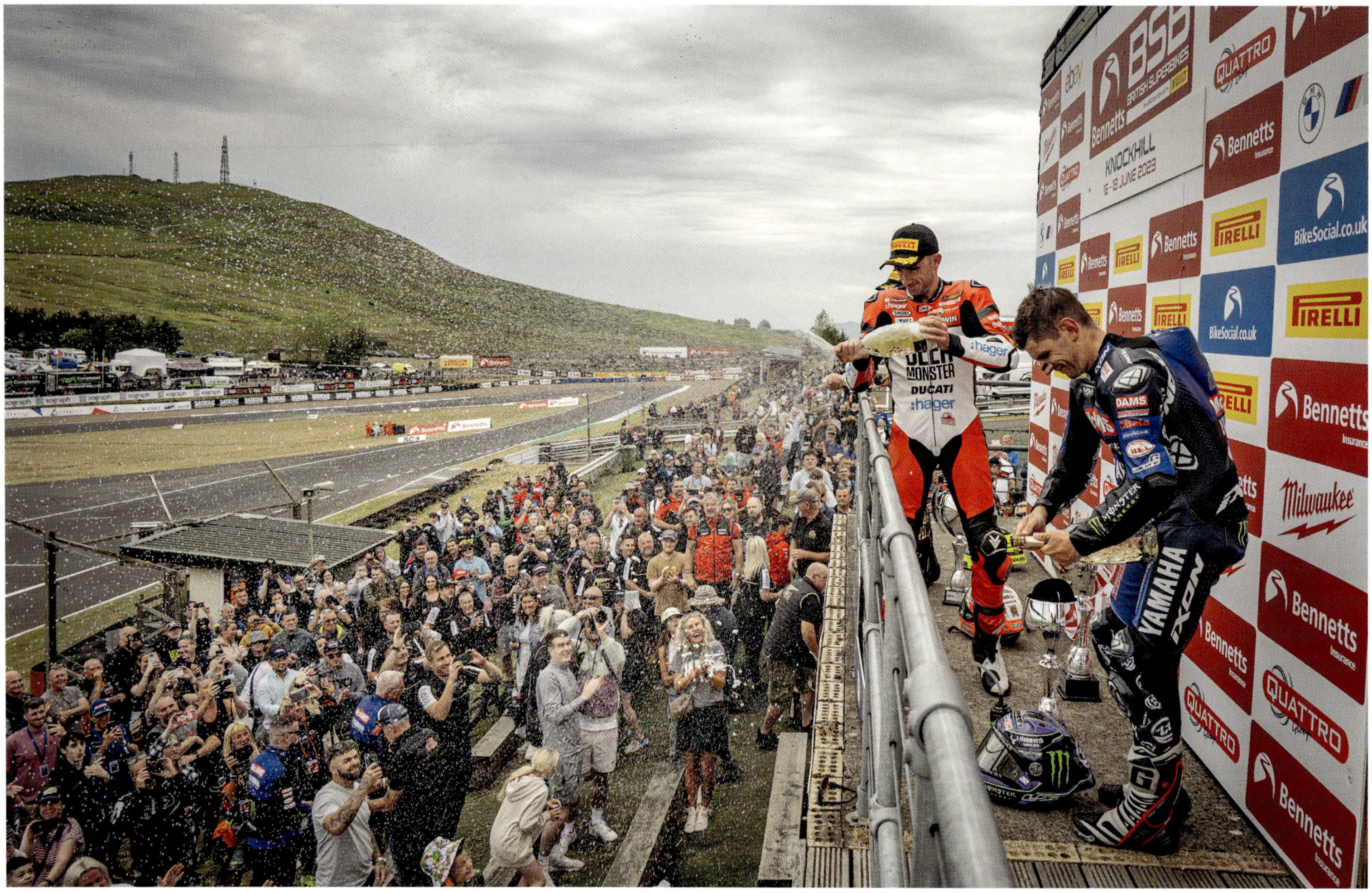
BSB
KNOCKHILL
16-18 JUNE 2023
Bennetts
PIRELLI
QUATTRO
BikeSocial.co.uk
Milwaukee
MONSTER
DUCATI
hager
YAMAHA

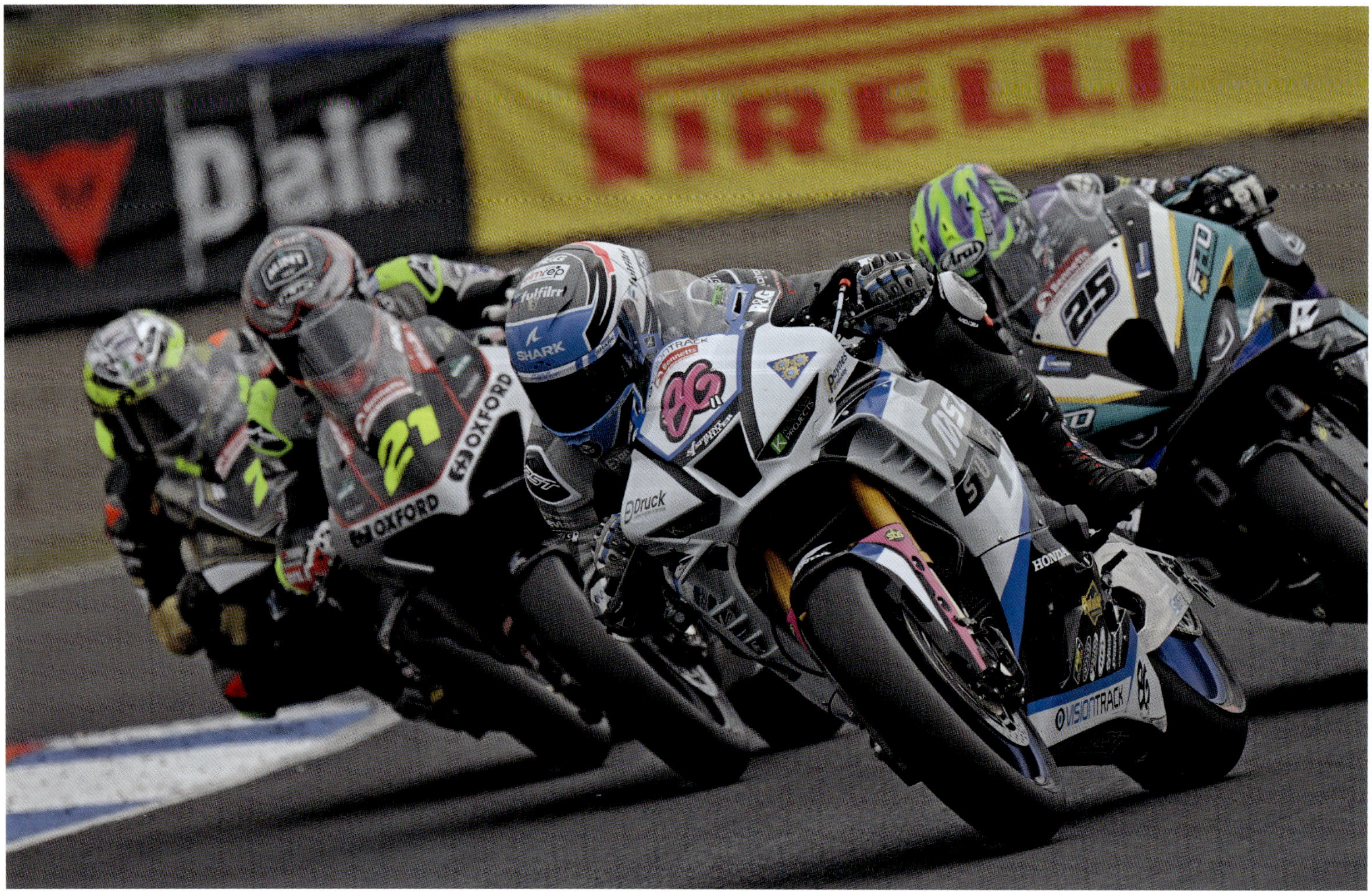
PIRELLI
OXFORD
SHARK
Druck
HONDA
VISIONTRACK
21
25

Closer to home, the Knockhill Motor Sports Club was organising both car and bike Scottish championship events headed up by president Niall Mackenzie, chairman Stuart Gray and key directors of the club Jillian Shedden and Gemma Hobbs with Dennis Hobbs and Alan Brunton playing primary roles on the bike sport side of things, and Rory Butcher, then Duncan Vincent, heading up the car side of the club. With the newly created Super Lap Scotland Championship, there was now a new bridging gap for track day drivers who wanted to compete but were not in a position to make the leap to full racing.

The events proved popular as they were linked with car shows such as the Paul Walker Tribute. These resulted in crowds of several thousands for club drivers to compete in front of, which was not previously the norm. The "Twin Track" format was created, giving competitors the opportunity to compete on two tracks at the one venue, on the one weekend. This proved popular with visiting rounds from the south, which in turn enhanced the content of meetings, resulting in the events becoming fully Motorsport UK licensed, rather than mixed with Hot Hatch content, which was how they had initially started.

Opposite, top: Glenn Irwin, Kyle Ryde and Jason O'Halloran get "busy with the fizzy" after a hard-fought Saturday race at the 2023 Bennetts British Superbikes. The podium was moved from the pitlane to the Circuit Office so that riders could interact with the fans and soak them with the buddly!

Opposite, bottom: Superbikes action is fast and furious as Charlie Nesbitt (86), Josh Brookes (25), Christian Iddon (21) and Ryan Vickers all battle over the same bit of tarmac as they launch out of the hairpin in 2023.

Top: Paul Bryden shows off his mighty ex Swedish mid-engined Touring Car during the KMSC ModSports races. He campaigns the car locally and throughout the UK, usually with success wherever he races.

Bottom: Gemma Hobbs is the Knockhill Events Manager and is an integral part of the Knockhill Motor Sports Club too as she oversees all the bike racing activities.

Chapter 8: The Fifth Decade

The KMSC bike scene continued to be strong with riders such as Bruce Birnie, Donald MacFadyen, the Gilfillan brothers Sean and Greg, Mark Grigor and Willie Monie all featuring in the ultra-competitive Superbike and Clubman's class. Elsewhere in the other classes, riders such as Finn Chalk, Harry Pullar, Craig Shirlaw and Lewis Paterson would all feature strongly across the classes. It was the Scottish Sidecars that would see the biggest turnaround with the backing of Marin, who funded the entries of all riders, whether they raced at Knockhill or East Fortune. This funding resulted in capacity grids at both circuits, the likes of which had not been seen before.

Knockhill had always had a long association with the McRae family, from the earliest times with Jimmy McRae on the Super Special Stages of the Scottish Rally, through to the numerous visits by Colin McRae as he tested his latest rally car, bike or developed his R4 rally car. With such a strong link, it was thought that the 20th anniversary of Colin winning the World Rally Championship should be marked and a bespoke rallying weekend created. And so the first McRae Rally Challenge happened in 2015 with many of the McRae family present, twenty-two of Colin's competition cars on display and World Champions such as Stig Blomqvist, Hannu Mikkola, Derek Ringer and Robert Reid present. The event was much admired, and although it was not a financial success for the crcuit, a second event marking the 25th anniversary of Colin's win was planned for 2020. Sadly the Covid-19 pandemic struck and the celebrations were delayed two years.

Previous page: Formula Ford 1600 has been a mainstay of any car race meeting in Scotland, both at Ingliston and at Knockhill, with many top drivers experiencing the cut and thrust of close open-wheel racing. Here, Michael Gray (the 2022 Scottish champion) leads Ciaran Haggerty in a closely fought race a few years before he eventually clinched the title, which sadly marked the last time the Formula Fords ran in Scotland.

Opposite, top: Andy Forrest is one of the best racing car builders in the country; he has campaigned some of the most outrageous competition cars ever seen. Here he competes in "Storm Tropper", a fabulous Super Lap Scotland and TimeAttack winning car.

Opposite, bottom: Lee Crawford and Scott Hardie have been very successful in sidecar racing for years. The whole sidecar scene is indebted to the sponsorship of Marin, who have underwritten all the entry fees at Knockhill and East Fortune in recent seasons, bringing full grids back to every round.

Top left: The largest-ever collection of Colin McRae cars in Scotland was gathered for the inaugural McRae Rally Challenge in 2015. Twenty-three of "Colin's Cars" were on displayand on the track. An impressive and emotional sight.

Top right: From the earliest to the last of Colin's Cars, all were on view for fans to appreciate at the McRae Rally Challenge.

Bottom: A history-making moment. Max McRae re-enacts the famous Colin McRae celebratory "donuts" with Hollie McRae holding the same Saltire that Derek Ringer held in 1995.

Chapter 8: The Fifth Decade   139

The British Superbikes were enjoying some good years of racing with a strong headline grid of BSB riders, but in 2017 an additional feature was added: the Scotland versus England Yamaha Legends Challenge race! Sixteen of the best riders ever from Scotland took on their counterparts from England on identical RD 250 LCs. The biggest achievement was coaxing Naill Mackenzie out of retirement one more time to captain the Scottish team – an unmissable opportunity that he jumped at! The two teams as listed below.

After captaining the winning team, Niall Mackenzie promised himself and his family that this was his last ever race and he would not be coming out of retirement for the third time. It was a fitting way to round off a sensational career, winning his final race on the same track he'd won his first!

Team Scotland

Niall Mackenzie (Captain)   Brian Morrison
Iain MacPherson   Joe Tonner
Donnie McLeod   Iain Duffus
John Crawford   Sandy Christie

Winning rider – Niall Mackenzie

Team England

Alan Carter (Captain)   Andy Muggleton
Curt Langan   Geoff Fowler
Dave Crampton   Graeme Mitchell
Dale Robinson   Charlie Corner

Winning team – Scotland

Left: Jim McRae provided his services as the opening car at the inaugural McRae Rally Challenge in 2015. In 2022 he was to compete directly against his son Alister and grandson, Max.

Below: The eyes have it! In this case, the distinctive eyes of Prince William look out of the Extreme E rally car during his visit to Knockhill in May 2021.

Chapter 8: The Fifth Decade   141

Right: The life and contribution of both David Leslie Snr and Jnr was marked on the 50th anniversary of Formula Ford when a mass gathering of previous Scottish champions assembled on the grid around the Leslies' famous Royale FF1600.

During this time, the Knockhill management team had engaged in numerous activities that had directly or indirectly supported the armed forces and their benevolent funds. The Ministry of Defence had created a bronze, silver and gold covenant scheme, recognising companies that support both serving members of the armed forces and veterans across the three services. Having achieved the bronze and silver awards, it was in 2019 that the Knockhill circuit was awarded the Gold Covenant for services and support of the armed forces. This is the highest award from the armed forces that can be given to companies and it was bestowed at the National Army Museum, at the Chelsea Barracks in London, by Chief of Defence Staff Sir Nicholas Carter, with the circuit being one of only a hundred companies in the UK to receive it that year.

In 2022, the circuit was in a position to host the second running of the McRae Rally Challenge, postponed from 2020, which proved to be particularly special with three generations of the McRae family competing directly against each other. Grandfather Jimmy entered the famous Stobart Ford Escort which already had so much previous McRae rallying pedigree, Alister entered in the same Hyundai Accent WRC he had previously rallied, and young Max stepped up to a Ford Fiesta Rallye 2. It proved to be a special event as it was attended by ex-World, European and British champions from the sport as well as six-time Olympic gold medallist Sir Chris Hoy making his rally debut.

After a long and hugely committed time as the owner of Knockhill, it was time for Derek Butcher to take a well-earned back seat. His almost forty years of ownership had as many twists and turns as the Knockhill track itself, and the progress in that time was there for all to see, in the circuit, the facilities and the sound footing of the business itself. It was, without doubt, a labour of love, that love being motorsport. And, fortunately, the succession plan for Knockhill had already been in place for some years.

The official transition of ownership from Derek Butcher to his daughter Jillian Shedden happened in February 2020 and then, in March, Covid-19 struck! The circuit management team were well aware of the impact of Covid-19 on local hospitals and on the weekend of 21 and 22 March, the circuit was due to run a track day followed by testing. Saturday happened but by Sunday morning, the situation had escalated overnight and the decision was taken to voluntarily close the gates to competitors who were due to test that day. All were understanding and within hours, the entire nation was instructed by the government to stay at home.

With the circuit closed, Jillian had the biggest challenge on her hands since the circuit was built almost five decades before. The business was shut down for an unknown period of time, just as the 2020 season was starting. All staff were furloughed and gates remained locked for week after week. Thankfully things slowly reopened, firstly track days, followed by events, followed by driving experiences because of the need for social distancing. A limited selection of events ran, the BSB did not come to Knockhill owing to Covid-19 travel restrictions between Scotland and England and the BTCC ran behind closed doors. It was a very challenging year!

Left: Celebrating in style! Danny Buchan (left), Jake Dixon (centre) and Leon Haslam (right) strike a pose. The podium finishers were often taken to interact with fans at the hairpin so they can taste the champagne too!

One surprising early visitor after the circuit slowly reopened in May 2021 was its first Royal visitor, Prince William, who was invited to drive the ProDrive-developed Extreme E rally car. After multiple Zoom meetings and visits by local police, search dogs and the Metropolitan Police from London, Prince William arrived with his entourage and drove the rally car twice, once in the 4x4 car park to get used to the car and then a proper "blast" on the rallycross stage. Who would have thought all those years ago that a senior member of the Royal family would be testing an electric rally car on the Knockhill rallycross track!

In 2021, with the pandemic still ongoing, a maximum crowd of 4,000 was agreed with the Scottish Government, but this had to be reduced to 1,000 just ten days before the event. Thankfully, the majority of fans retained their tickets for the 2022 event, and with Scottish riders Tarran Mackenzie and Rory Skinner both fighting for race wins, the interest in the event more than made up for the disappointment and challenges of the previous two years. Both men featured on the podium, much to the enjoyment of the patriotic fans, before moving on to the WSB and Moto GP paddocks respectively in 2023.

In 2023, life at Knockhill was fully back to normal for spectators, with Irish rider Andrew Irwin featuring as the star rider at the BSB event. Without any Scottish stars on the grid, local interest would turn to the lower classes with local riders Lennon Docherty and Oliver Barr flying the Saltire high, with Lennon scoring a brace of wins and Oliver winning one race. It's clear that these two riders show real signs of becoming the stars of the future.

Top: Knockhill's first royal visitor was Prince William in May 2020 at a press event when he drove the Extreme E electric rally car ahead of the delayed Scottish event in 2023. Prince William stayed longer than planned and proved a real hit with the Knockhill team.

Bottom: Rising star Lennon Docherty did "the double" at the 2023 British Superbikes event by winning both rounds of the Junior Supersport Championship.

Top: Knockhill's largest corporate booking to date was the world launch of the Porsche Caymen GT4. Porsche Germany booked out Knockhill for fourteen days and flew journalists in from all over the world to drive the new model; hosted by Mark Webber and Walter Rhorl.

Bottom: A British Superbikes pre-event PR visit was to Broomhall House to meet Lord Bruce (center). Tommy Bridewell, Tarran Mackenzie and Series Director, Stuart Higgs, learned all about Scottish history during their visit.

Chapter 8: The Fifth Decade

Opposite: Scottish strongman Andy Black has become a regular attendee at the Knockhill show events. His amazing demonstrations of strength. Certainly appeal to the family audiences!

Below: Brothers-in-law in close action on the track in 2021 as Rory Butcher (6) leads Gordon Shedden on the approach to McIntyre's.

Next page: The newest and biggest addition to the event calendar is the November Live Action Family Fireworks event. It immediately became a hit for old and young alike as it combines 4 hours of track action and one of the biggest fireworks displays in the country. Here the trucks join in the fun as a taster for the 2023 SuperTruck Scotland event.

152 Knockhill: 50 Years of Racing

Investment in the venue has always been at the forefront of the management team's approach and this has continued apace with a further resurface of the entire track and investment in new technology. With ever-increasing safety standards being required, FIA Formula 1-style safety lights and fibre optic cabling was installed around the whole circuit.

In April 2023, the latest addition to the venue became the acquisition of "The View" hospitality centre overlooking the hairpin exit. The View is an ex-Formula 1 hospitality unit and it is hoped it will be a catalyst and a "gamechanger" for Knockhill, as it will be used for a multitude of different reasons midweek, as well as being used as a site for hospitality at weekend events. This proved to be only a brief addition to the facilities at Knockhill as it was sold later that summer.

As we reflect on the first fifty years at Knockhill, it's fair to say that the circuit is almost unrecognisable now when we compare it to how it was in those early years. It has gone from a muddy track in the countryside with a couple of buildings to Scotland's National Motorsport Centre, a venue fit for the modern world. The vision of the early pioneers has been realised by Derek Butcher and his incredibly dedicated team, all of whom have been key to the successful circuit we see and use today. It is a remarkable achievement and we can now look forward with huge optimism to what the years ahead may bring for Knockhill.

Opposite, top: Car versus bike: which is fastest? Even in the wet, the bike out drags were one of the fastest accelerating production cars made. Here, Willie Monie outpaces Alan Stamper in his Porsche 911 Turbo S.

Opposite, bottom: Colin Miller, the "Flyin Fifer", has been a star at family events with his "1250hp" Ford, with an additional 800hp courtesy of nitrous oxide! The sheer power can be guaranteed to wow young and old alike.

Above: Rallycross has enjoyed a return in recent years with the re-establishment of the rallycross circuit. The Darlington and District Motor Club now run an annual season-closing event in October, reliving the earliest days of Knockhill, but this time on a surface that is fit for purpose.

PART THREE

50 Years in Pictures

Previous page: Going up with a bang! Working with 21CC Edinburgh Fireworks, one of the largest firework display companies in Scotland, the annual November event is a fine way to round off a sporting season.

Above: Takuma Sato leaves a plume of spray behind him during the British Formula 3 Championship round in 2001. He later had great success in America, winning the Indy 500 in 2017 and in 2020.

Opposite: The first of the images from Jim Moir's personal collection after years of taking photos at Knockhill.

Chapter 9
Jim Moir

50 Years Through One Man's Lens

Edinburgh-based photographer Jim Moir has been taking motorsport photographs at Knockhill since its opening ceremony on 22 September 1974. Here are his recollections on how photography has changed over those five decades, along with a selection of his favourite images. We hope you enjoy Jim's photographic journey.

They say time passes quickly when you're enjoying yourself and the last fifty years have certainly flown by.

Coming from Bo'ness, and having a father interested in both cars and photography meant annual visits to Bo'ness Hill Climb and many hours in the attic at home afterwards producing postcard prints on a Jumbo enlarger, illuminated with a handheld lamp. My interest grew as Ingliston Circuit opened in 1965 and I became more involved through a magazine called *Scottish Clubman*, which was produced monthly by a group of enthusiasts and edited by Fred Stephen in Stonehaven. It covered all forms of car and bike sport in Scotland, and I sent the editor a set of photographs taken at Ingliston with my Praktica SLR and 200mm Hanimex lens to see if they were of interest. It transpired that they were looking for a photographer to cover Ingliston meetings and offered me the job. This enabled me to qualify for a press pass, which helped enormously with access.

Two of the contributing journalists were Joanna Thomson and Chris McGuigan and they wrote for *Motoring News*, who also happened to be looking for a photographer to cover race meetings. I took on that role with *Motoring News*, which continues today. And with Knockhill opening in 1974, this offered even more scope for photography.

Left: A happy race winner: Tom Ingram being interviewed by ITV's Louise Goodman at the BTCC meeting in 2017.

Below: Another icon of Motorsport, Sir Stirling Moss donning his period helmet as he demonstrates the Vanwall replica at the SpeedFair meeting in 2007.

Chapter 9: Jim Moir

In those days everything was taken on film and I had graduated to a Nikkormat SLR and 300mm lens, which was handier for Knockhill as the track was wider and photographers were placed further back from the action. Getting images to *Motoring News* in London meant going home from a meeting with six rolls of Kodak Tri-X, developing them and then blacking out the kitchen to print a dozen or so images. I then drove to Edinburgh Airport the following morning to put them on the 08.00 British Airways shuttle to Heathrow where they were collected by Shand Press Services and couriered to *Motoring News'* offices in the City. There were few security issues and handing over an envelope at the BA desk for sending as an air letter was simple and involved only a cursory look at the contents by a staff member. Eventually, security issues did put a stop to this method and it became more difficult to get material to them down in London. Often, however, there would be a driver or team from the south at a meeting and *Motoring News* would arrange for them to take the film with them for collection the following morning.

Right: Ben Mason dominated the Legends series in 2005, 2006 and 2007.

Below: Oops! The SMRC Mini Cooper Cup has always been fast and furious; it offers some of the closest racing in the UK.

Opposite, bottom: Visiting Fiestas at the BRSCC meeting in 2022. The kerbing and camber angles at the chicane during reverse direction meetings often provide an interesting shot.

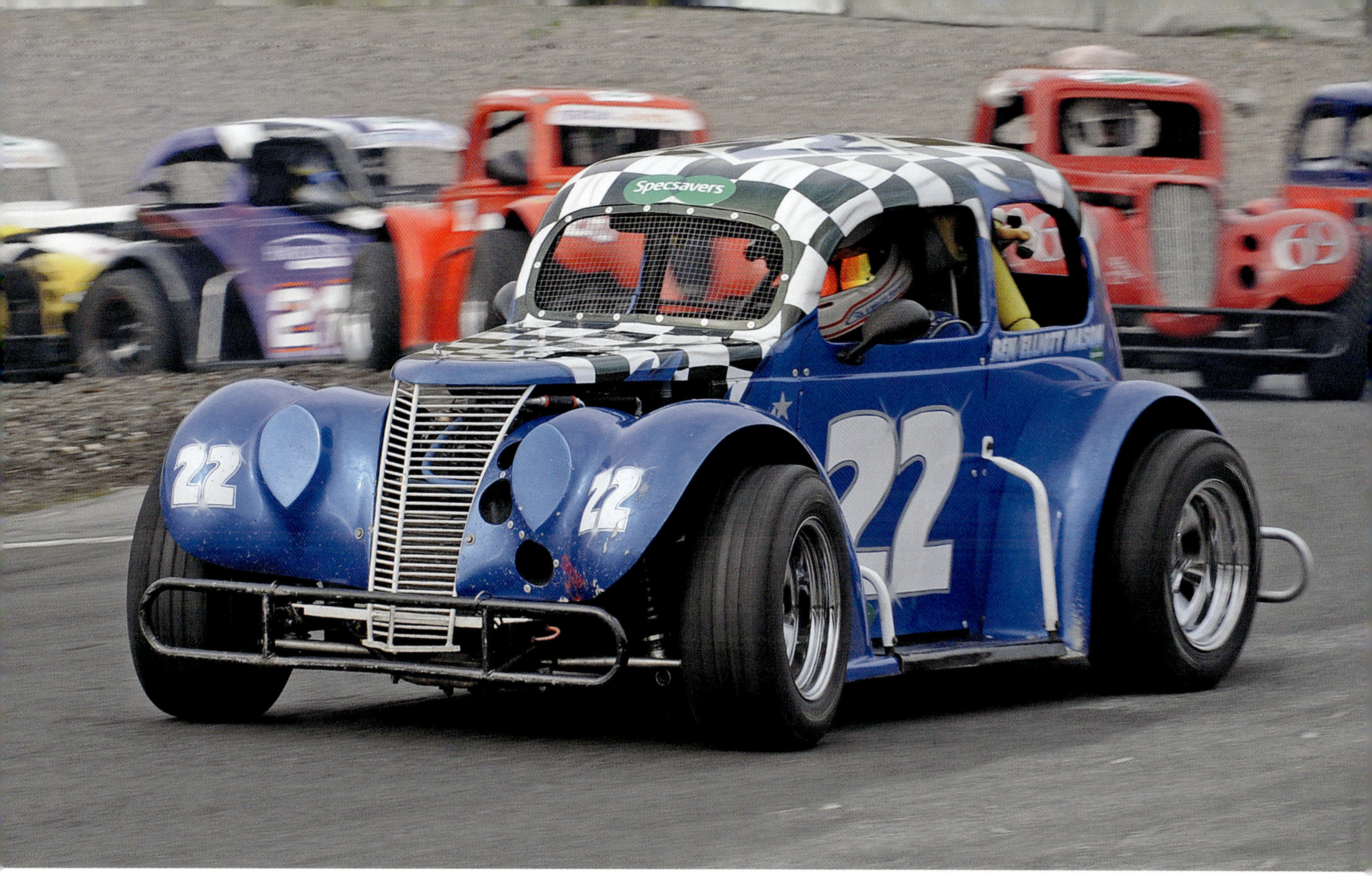
Specsavers
22
22
22

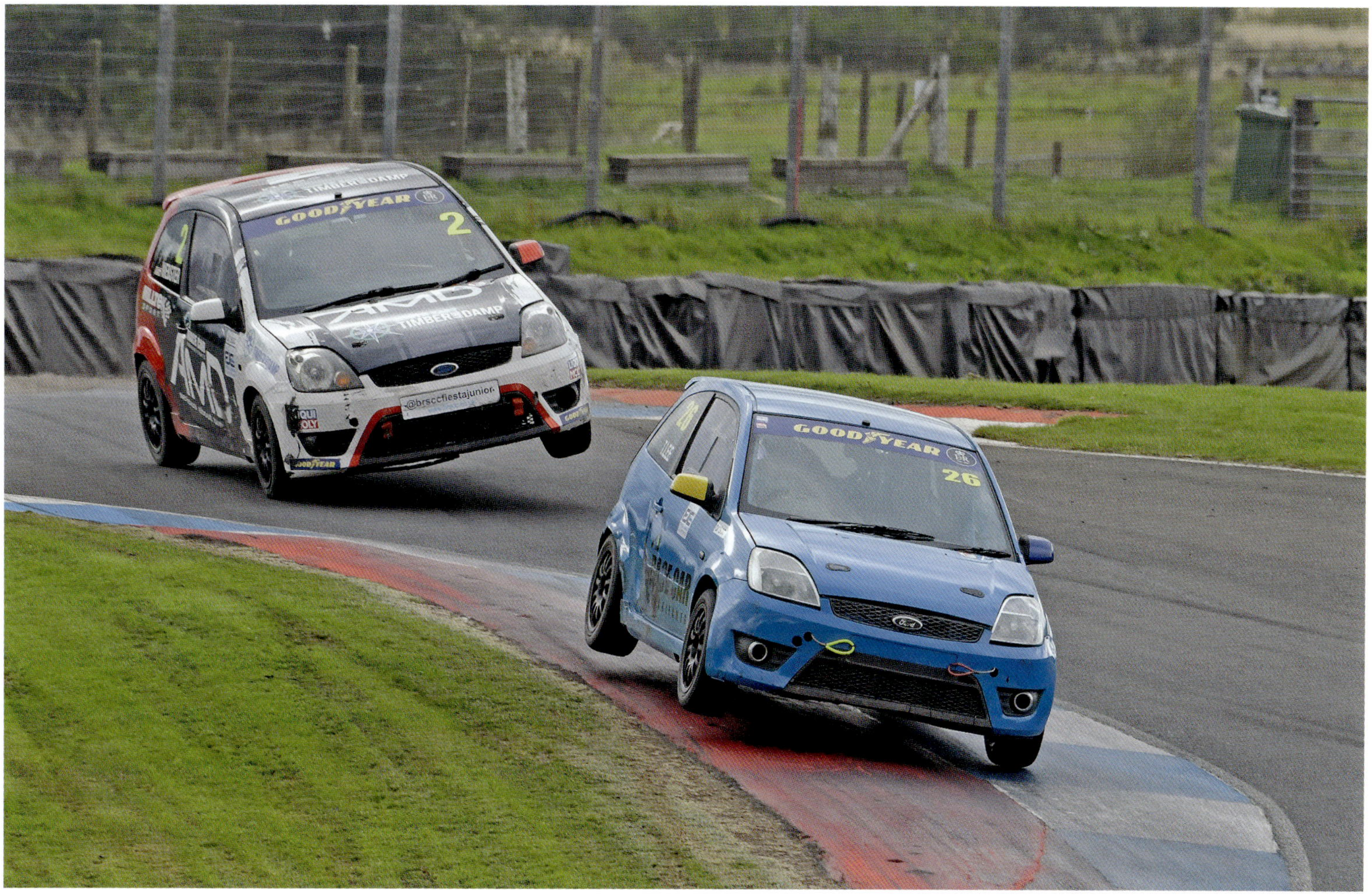
GOODYEAR
2
GOODYEAR
26

After Bill Henderson retired from *Autosport* magazine, his place as a photographer was taken by Graeme Brown. Graeme was a bit more up to speed with modern technology than I was; he had a negative scanner and computer which enabled him to send images electronically to *Autosport*. He kindly offered to scan my negs and send them to *Motoring News,* which in practice meant taking a developing kit to Knockhill and using one of the paddock garages that had running water to develop my films. I then dried them with a hair dryer, marked the ones for *Motoring News* and gave them to Graeme for scanning and sending off.

It was clear that I had to move on and get more up-to-speed with modern technology. I was now using colour film and a Nikon F5 autofocus camera, which made tracking a fast-moving car a bit easier. I was doing work for the SMRC and also for Laurance Laybourne, who had a printing company and sponsored the Fiesta series at Knockhill. Laurance produced a high-quality newsletter on the series along with the SMRC magazine, *Wheelspin*, and the Knockhill race programmes. I was supplying prints for these publications, but Laurance then offered me one of their old Mac computers to which I added a scanner and modem and thus the move to digital progressed.

Opposite: Two icons of Scottish Motorsport: David Leslie Snr, who was instrumental in guiding the early careers of several top Scottish drivers, including David Coulthard, Allan McNish and Dario Franchitti, watches son David preparing to compete in his classic Royale FF car at the SpeedFair meeting in 2006.

Above: Scottish FF Champion 2019 and 2021, Jordan Gronkowski reflected in action on the rain-soaked track.

> "It was clear that I had to move on and get more up-to-speed with modern technology. I was now using colour film and a Nikon F5 autofocus camera, which made tracking a fast-moving car a bit easier."

Chapter 9: Jim Moir

Left: Liam McGill cocks two wheels as he heads down Duffus Dip.

Below: Caterhams cresting Duffus.

Opposite, top: Anything you can do, I can do better: two Mini racers go for some big air!

Opposite, bottom: Is this racing or rallycross? Competitors are trying out both for size during a Mini Cooper race.

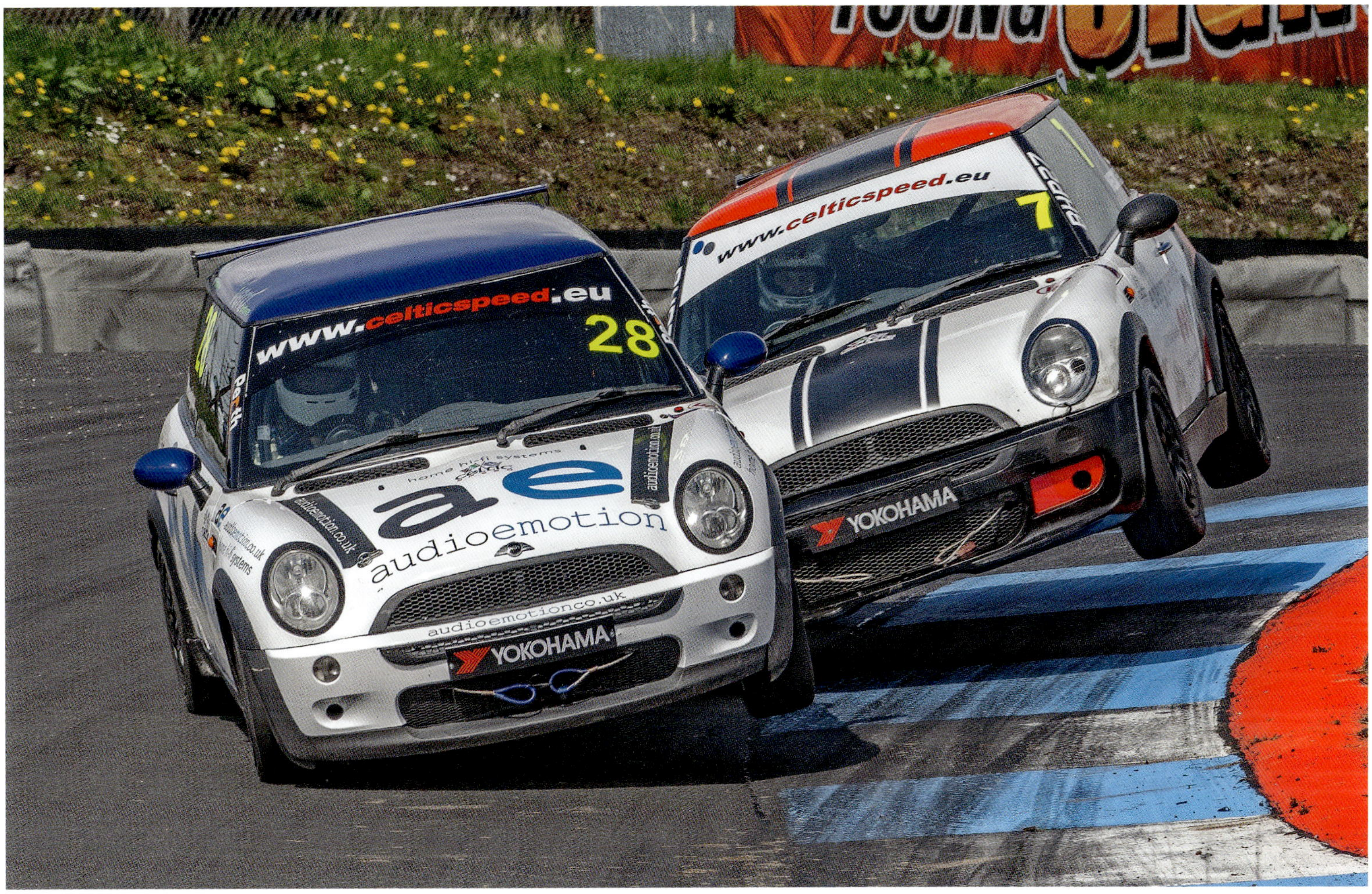
www.celticspeed.eu
28
ae
audioemotion
YOKOHAMA
www.celticspeed.eu
7
YOKOHAMA

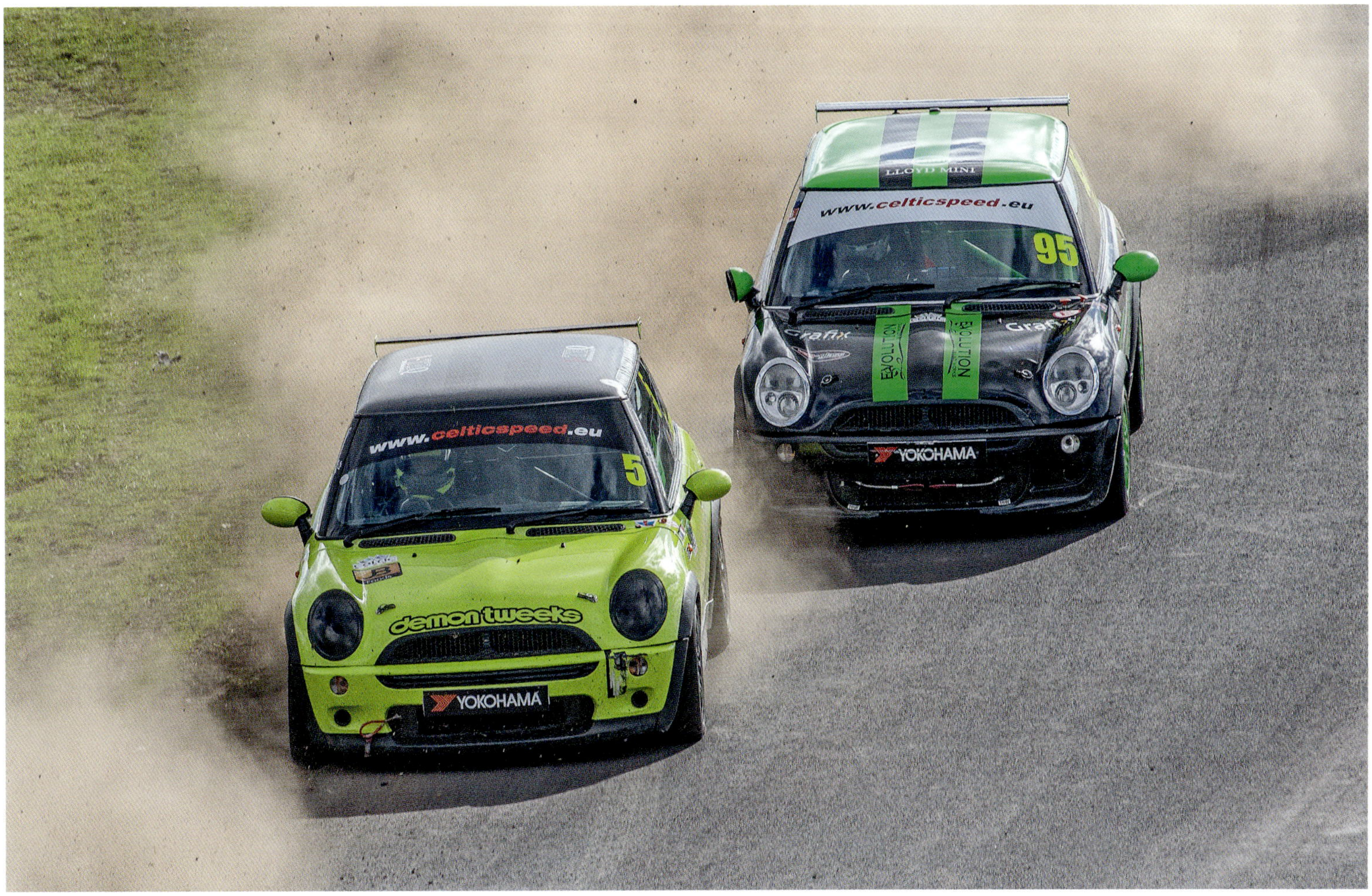
www.celticspeed.eu
95
YOKOHAMA
www.celticspeed.eu
5
demon tweeks
YOKOHAMA

Above: Rory Butcher has raced a wide variety of cars at Knockhill and Jim Moir's lens has brilliantly captured them all at some point.

Right: Scottish Formula Ford rivals Craig Brunton and Kenneth Thirwell go wheel-to-wheel!

> **"I've hugely enjoyed my time working at Knockhill, covering such a wide variety of events, and I very much hope you enjoy this personal selection of my photographs taken from the last fifty years."**

Graeme had moved on to work for Castrol, covering the Superbike series and around the same time *Autosport* bought *Motoring News* and rebranded it *Motorsport News*. I then took on the *Autosport* role as well and bought my first fully digital camera, an ex-rental Nikon D1, along with an autofocus Nikon 300mm F2.8 lens and a 1.4 converter. I still have this lens and, despite its age, it remains a superb performer. Not needing to print saved a lot of time and avoided the necessity of constantly blacking out the kitchen or bathroom. This pleased my wife no end!

Subsequently, over the years I have used a number of Nikon cameras, all now digital. With increasing safety requirements at UK tracks, photographers now have to work further back from the track and, in some cases, certain areas at corners are out of bounds. This results in photographers needing longer lenses and I now use a 200-500mm zoom with which I can cover most eventualities. Cameras now have connectivity with mobile phones and tablets et cetera, normally via Bluetooth. With social media requirements being almost immediate nowadays, this means that at the end of a race, everything shot is on my mobile and can be emailed off to Facebook or whoever.

I've hugely enjoyed my time working at Knockhill, covering such a wide variety of events, and I very much hope you enjoy this personal selection of my photographs taken from the last fifty years.

Jim Moir, November 2023

Above: Framed! A Dunlop tyre technician hard at work at the BTCC meeting 2018.

Left: A study in concentration.

Opposite: Racer Stevie McCreight wrestles with his leathers following a hot session on track!

Chapter 10
Steven Mackay

A Year in the Life of Knockhill

Above: Pre-race contemplation! Bike racer, Luke Stapleford, surveys his competition ahead of going into battle.

Right: At a lean angle. Club racer, Sean McTaggart, on the power through Clark's corner.

Steven Mackay:
His Royal Photographic Society portfolio

As a keen photographer, Steven Mackay used the skills and techniques he learned photographing motorsport at Knockhill to become an Associate of the Royal Photographic Society. Thereafter, with a view to progressing further, Steven approached Knockhill and asked if he could take some behind the scenes images for a future Royal Photographic Society portfolio submission.

In contrast to his previous photographs, which were primarily track based, the proposed project would focus exclusively on what makes Knockhill tick, namely the staff, competitors and spectators. Consequently, during the 2022 season, Steven was given unprecedented access to the circuit, where he captured a range of images that illustrates how people make Knockhill the unique, diverse and truly exciting place that it is.

We hope you enjoy this collection of black and white images, which Steven has dubbed "Knockhill's super staff to superstars".

Top: A change in career? Sir Chris Hoy made his rally debut at the 2022 McRae Rally Challenge.

Middle: Awaiting instructions! Caterham racing is fast and furious with last minute instructions always an advantage for the driver.

Bottom: Happy at your work! Tiziano about to make last minute preparations ahead of an event.

Opposite, top: A very tyring business. Tyre fitting at events is a relentless job as riders chase for lap times on new tyres.

Opposite, bottom: Ace rally navigator Clare Mole gets ready for the McRae Rally Challenge in 2022.

Chapter 10: Steven Mackay 173

Top: Hannah Chapman of Rennat Design contemplates her next race helmet creation.

Middle: Final checks. This bike racer checks his tyre warmers are up to temperature.

Bottom: Contemplation before a race!

Left A star in the making. Ace racer Rory Skinner is happy with how things went at the 2022 British Superbikes meeting.

Below: Easter fun day. Easter egg rolling at Duffus Dip is always a hit with the kids.

Bottom: A pair of wise old hands preps a grandchild's Mini Moto.

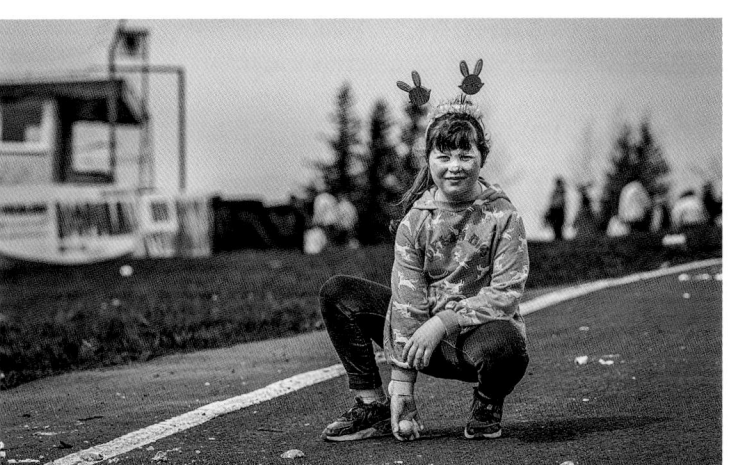

Left: Total concentration. The boss of Rennat Designs, Joe Tanner, applies the finishing touches to another top helmet design creation.

Below: Awaiting the off. Eugene McManus waits for his call to action.

Opposite, top: A helping hand. Motorsport is all about teamwork. Here, Kyle Ryde gets a shove to go on track.

Opposite, middle: The finishing touches. It's always important to present the circuit at its best.

Opposite, bottom right: Car racer, Chloe Grant, prepares for a pre-season test day.

Opposite, bottom left: The kids play park at the Kart Centre is always a popular hangout for the next generation.

Chapter 10: Steven Mackay 177

Top left: Long-time team member Kirstin Forrest helps prep the Knockhill circuit for one of its major events.

Top right: Events manager Gemma Hobbs leads hundreds on to the track for the annual egg rolling at Duffus Dip as part of the Easter family fun day.

Right: The eyes have it! Graham Whitehill watches the track action to keep everyone safe.

Opposite: A name to watch! A very young David Coulthard visited Knockhill before starting his Formula 1 career.

Chapter 11
Legends of Motorsport
Snaps of Racing Stars

Top left: 1995 World Rally Champion Colin McRae was a very regular visitor and always enjoyed entertaining the crowd.

Top right: John Hopkins was one of the most experienced racers ever to have competed at Knockhill with his successes in MotoGP, the World Superbike Championship, the American AMA Championship and the British Superbikes. A true star and always popular with the fans where ever he goes.

Bottom: Rivals reunited. Grand Prix stars Niall Mackenzie and Kevin Schwantz share a joke together at the 2002 British Superbikes event.

Opposite, top left: Alister McRae (left) and world bike stunt champion Kevin Carmichael enjoying a laugh together in the snow.

Opposite, top right: Ron Haslam has had a four decade association with Knockhill. He would compete during his stellar racing career, put his name to our Ron Haslam Honda Bike School in the 1990s and oversee his own son Leon's racing exploits. We are pleased that Ron and his wife Ann have had such a long relationship with Knockhill.

Opposite, bottom: A very early Formula 1 visitor was Martin Brundle (right) seen here with Derek Butcher just after he had purchased the circuit.

Chapter 11: Legends of Motorsport 181

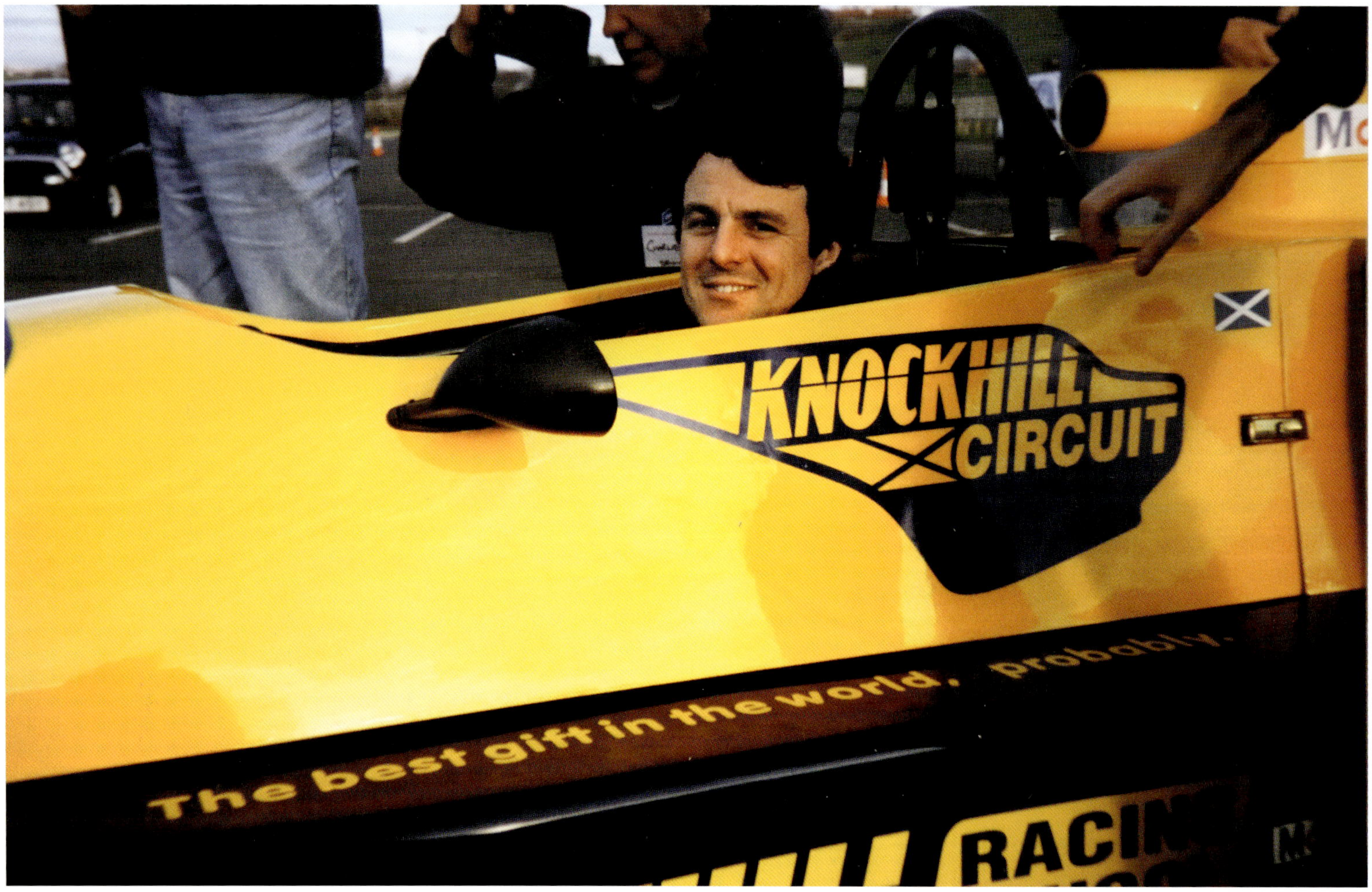
KNOCKHILL
CIRCUIT
The best gift in the world. probably.
RACIN

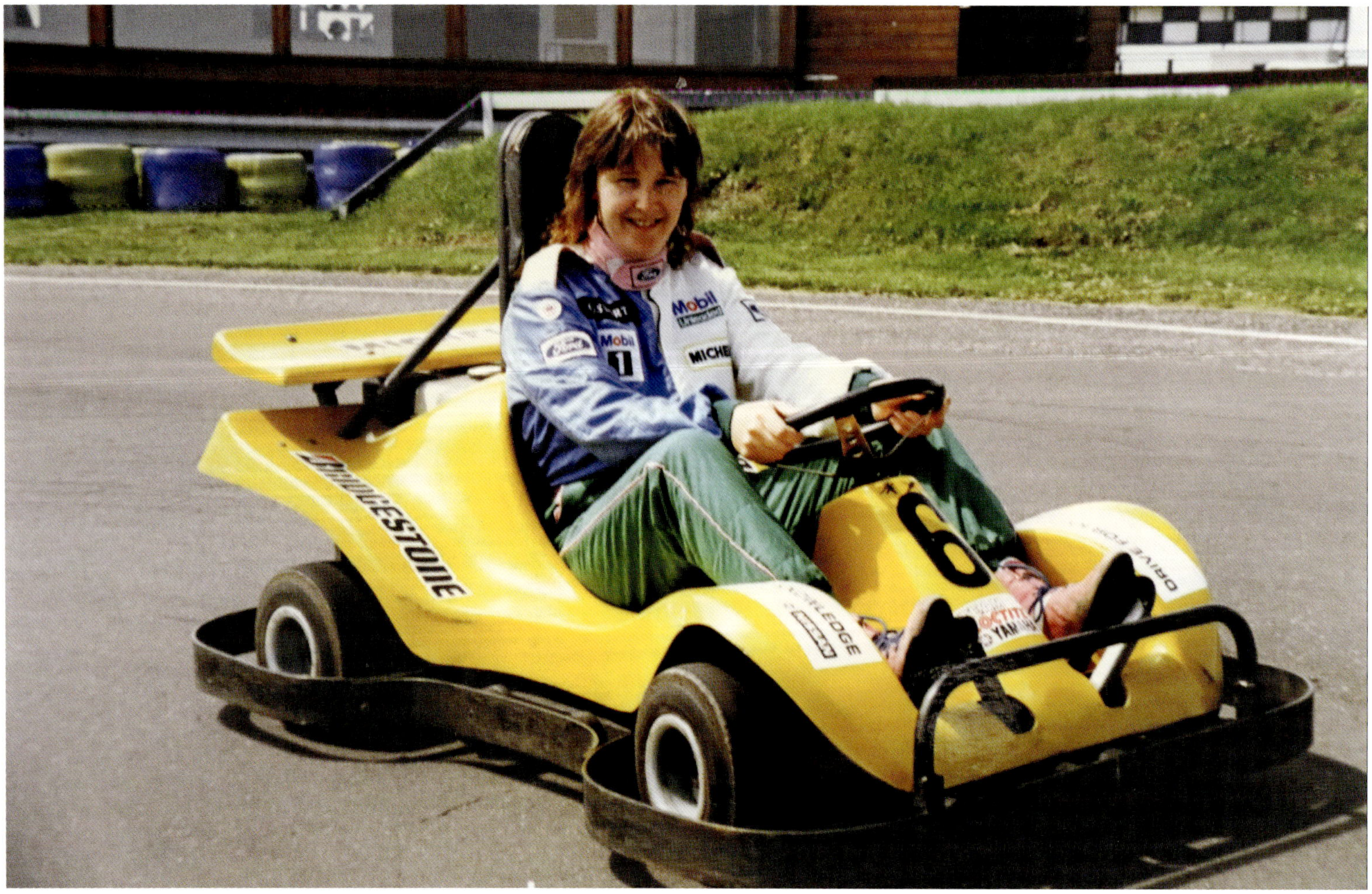
BRIDGESTONE
Mobil

Opposite, top: Formula 1 and Indy Car racer Mark Blundell paid a visit for a children's charity event in the early 1990s.

Opposite, bottom: World Rally Champion Louise Aitken-Walker having fun at the kart centre.

Top: Peter Hickman is fast becoming one of the greatest-ever riders at the Isle of Man TT and currently holds the outright lap record at a remarkable average speed of 136.358mph. He combines his road racing with the British Superbikes and you can tell where Peter is in the Knockhill paddock as there is always a huge crowd after his attention.

Bottom left: Frank Biela was a welcome returning racer to the non-championship David Leslie Super Touring event in 2016.

Bottom right: Moto2 rider Rory Skinner got dispensation to start racing at Knockhill at the age of eleven, such was his potential and successes at an early age. His stellar rise has been remarkable and has already made is make in the local, national and world scene. Here he receives the Steve Hislop Award from Stuart Gray after setting the fastest race lap at the 2022 Bennetts British Superbikes round.

Chapter 11: Legends of Motorsport 183

Top left: Suzie Wolff visited with the MUK "Dare to be Different" programme to encourage more girls and young women to get involved in motorsport.

Top right: Rallying legend Hannu Mikkola was a guest of honor at the 2015 McRae Rally Challenge.

Above: The McRae Rally Challenge in 2022 attracted a galaxy of stars. Pictured here are Gwyndaf Evans, Max McRae, Alister McRae and Elfyn Evans.

Right: The return of Super Touring to Knockhill in 2016 brought together former rivals Frank Biela, John Cleland and Gabriele Tarquini, together with members of the Leslie family.

Left: The bike-racing Dunlop family have achieved remarkable successes across road and circuit racing and the latest member to race at Knockhill has been Michael who competed on a GP125 before his remarkable successes at the Isle of Man TT.

Below: Former British and World Superbike Champion, and now TV and media pundit, Neil Hodgson was a crowd favourite and had great successes with his super smooth riding style.

Bottom: Tartan take-over! The British Superbike riders join in the Scottish theme at the Forth Bridge and put on kilts for a media shoot. Here John Hopkins, Tommy Hill, Shane Byrne, Laura Stevens (BSB Media and Communications), Josh Brookes and Jake Zemke are flanked by Duncan Vincent (left) and Stuart Gray (right).

Left: Dario Franchitti (right) is a regular visitor, as he keeps a close eye on the Scottish racing scene. Here he is thanking the marshals for their support.

Below: Le Mans winner and head of Audi Sport Allan McNish lends his support to the SMRC marshals by donning a set of orange overalls and seeing for himself the valuable contributions marshals make to delivering a race meeting safely.

Bottom: The original Stig at Knockhill! The legendary rally champion Stig Blomqvist took part in the 2015 McRae Rally Challenge in a Vauxhall Firenza but also did some demo laps in his beloved Audi Quattro Sport.

Top left: Steve Hislop was one of the greatest all round bikers racers with huge successes on the roads as well as circuit racing. His exploits are legendary and we are proud to have a corner named after him at Knockhill.

Top right: One of the most popular racers of all time is John McGuinness (right) with twenty-three TT wins to his name, seen here with Gordon Shedden. John is one of the instructors on the Niall Mackenzie Superbike Experience Track Days and likes nothing more than chatting with riders in the pit lane or over lunch and passing on his wealth of experience. A true legend in every way.

Left: Three generations of the McRae family together! Fourteen-year-old Max has just completed his BARS rally licence course with Bob Watson. Centre is grandfather Jimmy and right is Max's father Alister.

Chapter 11: Legends of Motorsport 187

Above: Twice British Touring Car Champion John Cleland took on the challenge of a Scottish Hill Rally event, which had a special stage at Knockhill.

Left: Taylor and Tarran Mackenzie pose in front of the Kelpies near Falkirk for a pre-BSB promo photo shoot.

Opposite: In 1987, Knockhill built a demanding motocross track in the centre of the circuit and hosted the British Championships.

Chapter 12
Thrills and Spills

And They Walked Away . . .

190 Knockhill: 50 Years of Racing

Opposite, top: Stunt rider Kevin Carmichael was a regular attender to woo the crowds at early Hot Hatch track day events.

Opposite, bottom: Terry Grant earliest display shows were at Knockhill, as the venue was one of the first to book him. This ongoing relationship has lasted over two decades.

Left: Full pull! Tractor pulling was a popular activity at Off Road Scotland, a show dedicated to the off-road and farming scene. The show would ultimately move to the Oatridge Agricultural Centre in West Lothian.

Below: Steve Murty's Pirelli wheelie truck was a popular performer at the first SuperTruck Scotland events in the early 1990s.

Bottom: Stunt riders began to be more extravagant with their stunts, particularly at the expense of their partner Craig Jones performs a "stoppie" at the 2006 Motor Fair.

Chapter 12: Thrills and Spills

Left and below: "Heat Wave" and the fire engine wheelie truck were creations of Steve Murty's, designed to entertain the crowds!

Opposite, top: "The Kangaroo Kid", Matt Coulter, was always a crowd pleaser with his daring quad jumps at the Hot Hatch Specacles in the early 1990s.

Opposite, bottom: A high-flying Harry King immediately became a fan favourite at the BTCC meetings in the Porsche Carrera Cup.

Chapter 12: Thrills and Spills   193

Above: Andy Forrest in his 7.2-litre twin turbo Westfield about to take on Bruce Burnie on his BMW RR 1000 Superbike. Who won? The car on this occasion.

Opposite: Entertaining the crows, stunt rider Kevin Carmihael and Shane Lynch go head to head at the hairpin.

Chapter 12: Thrills and Spills 195

Top: Knockhill has the reputation of being one of the most thrilling and spectacular circuits in the world to race on. This is a result of a combination of the topography and gradients of the circuit but also the aggressive use of the kerbs by some drivers which can cause cars to literally fly as they chase fast laps.

Above: David Leslie had a major off at the corner that is now called "Leslie's" at an early Touring Car meeting. Check out the size of the crowd, the championship was already huge in the early 1990s.

Left: One of the first one-make championships to come north was the MGF Championship, which always provided close racing – sometimes too close!

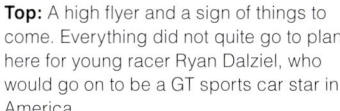

Top: A high flyer and a sign of things to come. Everything did not quite go to plan here for young racer Ryan Dalziel, who would go on to be a GT sports car star in America.

Above: Over and out! Mini racing has been one of the closest racing formula in recent times, but it doesn't always end well!

Right: Ashleigh Morris had a fairly sizeable "off" at the Grant Rally Stages in her beloved "JIG" Ford Fiesta. Thankfully, car and driver returned to rallying fairly soon afterwards.

Chapter 12: Thrills and Spills 197

Top: Wattie Brown crashes while exiting the hairpin and crashed again when he tried to restart his bike. Here, he gives a hands-up signal to show he is okay and also to signal "I give up!"

Middle: Top racer Joe Toner comes a cropper at the hairpin but thankfully slides out of harm's way.

Bottom: How not to take Duffus Dip! An unfortunate British Formula 4 racer takes a tumble down the hill.

Above: Ouch! Long-time racer Ron Cumming takes a nasty tumble at the hairpin. Thankfully, he was back to race at the very next meeting.

Right: Bike racer Dennis Hobbs was a guest driver in the SMRC Mini Cooper. Unfortunately all did not end well at Duffus Dip with an off. In practice and qualifying he was quick and on the front row against some top car racers.

Chapter 12: Thrills and Spills

Above and left: Marshals to the rescue! The SMRC and Scottish Bike marshals are among the best in the UK and always ready to help a competitor, whether on two wheels or four.

Opposite: Sir Ian Botham dropped in for a walking lap of the circuit as he walked from John O'Groats to Land's End in 1985. He's pictured here with PR man Raymond Smith.

Chapter 13
Celebrity Visitors

Guests from Stage, Screen and Sport

Top right: TV presenter Carol Smilie was a regular visitor, as her husband Alex Knight raced in the SMRC Fiesta Championship.

Bottom: Knockhill teamed up with Ladbrokes to host a series of "football stars in a rally car" promotion. Undoubled star, and hit with all those on site, was Chris Kamara (left) who entertained everyone.

Right: Aberdeen and Scotland football star Alex McLeish tries out Knockhill's Formula First cars for size.

Top left: Scottish comedian Fred MacAulay was given the guest car in the Fiesta ST support race to the Touring Cars. He was fully trained up by the Knockhill Team and loved the experience!

Bottom left: Celebrity chef turned racer: Nick Nairn was one of several guest drivers in the Celtic Speed Mini Cooper at SMRC events.

Top right: Boyzone star Shane Lynch became a very regular visitor as he took up drifting in the British Drifting Championship in the early 1990s, he's pictured here with Raymond Smith.

Bottom right: Pop band, The Honeyz, dropped in to promote their latest album and enjoyed a spin around the circuit in this classic Healey 3000.

Chapter 13: Celebrity Visitors

Below: The reigning Miss Scotland Aisling Friel was a guest of the *Scottish Sun*, who sponsored the 2006 Scottish MotorFair.

Bottom: Cilla and Artie, of children's musical entertainment group The Singing Kettle dropped in to record a sketch for their show in 1999.

Right: TV star Keith Chegwin entertained the crowd at the Scottish MotorFair in his own inimitable style, here interviewing Jet Pack Man, Eric Scott.

Right: Legendary Scottish rugby superstar and renowned MND campaigner Doddie Weir dropped in to do the Rally Experience with his family, he's pictured here with Dennis Hobbs and Mikey Gray.

Below: As a huge motorsport fan and car racer himself, Sir Chris Hoy has been a long time admirer of the McRae family rally exploits, and in particular those of Colin in the World Rally Championship. In 2022 the offer was made to him to make his rally debut at the McRae Rally Challenge and Chris jumped at the opportunity! On hearing this, long time rally competitor Willie Paterson kindly lent Chris his Mitsubishi Evo IX and Chris went on and finished a creditable 40th overall with co-driver Roy Campbell.

PART FOUR

Memorable Moments

Previous page: The fastest vehicle ever to have circulated around Knockhill! Aberdonian Nathan Kinch demonstrated his ex-Rubens Barrichello Ferrari Formula 1 car at the 2006 Scottish MotorFair in a time of 41.3 seconds. The speed and sound of the V10 will remain with everyone who was there that day.

Above: Sally Walker (second from right), Tom Kinnaird's daughter visited with her family to meet the author and Derek Butcher (third from left) and Jillian Shedden (third from right). The restaurant in Paddock 1 has been renamed Kinnairds Bistro in memory of the founder of Knockhill.

Opposite: In 2023, Max McRae, nephew of Colin McRae, trained to become a regular instructor for the Driving Experiences. He joins a long line of top names who lend their skills and knowledge to members of the public keen to experience first-hand the magic of Knockhill.

Chapter 14
Did You Know?

Top Trivia from the Track

Over its five decades, there have been numerous events, visitors and happenings at Knockhill. Here is just a selection from over the years. How many do you know?

Scottish chart-topping singer/songwriter Amy Macdonald trained at Knockhill ahead of her appearance on BBC's *Top Gear*'s "A Star in a Reasonably-Priced Car". After several visits to Knockhill, she topped the leaderboard and became the second fastest driver of all time.

Customers who take part in the Knockhill Rally Experience in the fleet of Group N Ford Fiestas drive on parts of the same rally stage layout as used by the Grant Construction Scottish Tarmac Rally round and the McRae Rally Challenges. This gives drivers a real, authentic rally experience.

At the British Superbikes on 16 June 2017, sixteen legends from Scotland and England took part in the Pro-Am challenge on Yamaha RD 250 LCs. It was one of the highlights of the event, which saw Niall Mackenzie fight hard to win his last ever bike race on the same circuit that he won his first. Racing stars included Brian Morrison, Iain Simpson, Iain Duffus and Sandy Christie. Scotland were proud to win the event overall!

Maxi Jazz, the renowned singer/songwriter raced twice at Knockhill, in a Nissan Z and in an SMRC Mini Cooper guest car.

Knockhill was the venue for one of the most challenging record attempts – the longest Tunnel of Fire to be ridden through on a motorcycle. This Guinness Book of World Records distance was set by Stephen Brown (below) on 7 August 2003, when he achieved a remarkable 175 feet.

At the inaugural Classic SpeedFair in 2006, the guest of honour was Sir Jackie Stewart. His older brother Jimmy Stewart (above), also a former racing driver, attended as well. It was the only occasion in history that the two Stewart brothers were on the same track at the same time, both driving original Ecurie Ecosse cars from the 1950s.

Knockhill has hosted three 24-hour cycling events have been hosted for teams of riders and solos, all in aid of Sense Scotland. The events' three patrons were Mark Beaumont, Olympic champion; cycling gamechanger Graeme Obree and Scottish rugby legend Kenny Logan. Obree actually took part in the event himself with his son. The solo winner cycled continuously for 24 hours, covering in that time the equivalent distance of Knockhill to Silverstone nearly 400 miles away in the East Midlands.

On 26 June 2014, ahead of the Glasgow Commonwealth Games, the Queen's Ceremonial Torch, which had visited every Commonwealth country in the world, completed a lap of honour on the back of a 1000cc race bike, ridden by Derek Butcher and held aloft by Jillian Shedden.

One of the biggest challenges facing the management team was when the track surface broke up owing to severe rains, on the morning of the start of biggest event weekend of 2015, the British Superbikes. With thousands of spectators on site, and the track unusable, all contractor contacts were called upon and – incredibly – the track was up and running after lunchtime, with sections of it resurfaced.

On 7 September 2014, over 1000 bikers crossed the Forth Road Bridge in memory of a popular fallen road rider. The bikes then rode to Knockhill to complete a lap of honour, filling the track from end to end. An impressive and emotional sight for all.

In 2007 and 2009, the British Superbike Championship and the Knockhill team, working with Glasgow City Council, shut down George Square and turned it into a temporary racetrack to preview the up-and-coming Knockhill round. Eric, the Go Fast-sponsored Jet Pack Man featured both times; in 2007 flying around the Square at around ten metres off the pavement and, in 2009, his launch site was the roof of the City Chambers Building, flying at some fifty metres high and speeds of around 70mph! Despite being a legendary TT road rider and multiple winner, Iain Hutchinson managed to crash at 20mph!

Colin McRae made his car race debut at the first British Touring Car event in 1992 driving a ProDrive BMW M3. He infamously pushed Matt Neal off at the hairpin, to a cheer from the crowd, but to the anger of Matt's father Steve, who was seen chasing down Colin who by then was hiding in his motorhome!

Super Tourers, the heyday of British Touring Cars, returned in force in September 2018 with former British and World Touring Car Champion Gabriele Tarquini, twice champion John Cleland and 1995 BTCC Champion Frank Biela putting on a show for the fans.

Knockhill was a long-term supporter of the construction of the Jim Clark Museum in Duns. Ahead of the Jim Clark 50th anniversary event, the Forth Road Bridge was closed for 11 minutes to allow Jim's US Grand Prix-winning Lotus Formula 1 car (above), his Lotus Cortina, DKW and Goggomobil to be driven for the media and the thousands of fans who lined the northbound carriageway on 25 August 2014.

In 2016, Ladbrokes wanted a promotion like *Top Gear*'s top-rated "A Star in a Reasonably-Priced Car", using big-name celebrities from Scottish football, SKY and the sports media world. So, the Knockhill team devised "A Football Star in a Rally Car" with Rory Butcher in the lead role assisted by senior rally instructor Bob Watson. On more than five occasions, the full media team from Ladbrokes brought along numerous high-profile players, managers and pundits to be tested with football questions by Rory, while they drove a rally car! The football stars included Ally McCoist, Willie Miller, Scott Brown, and the biggest laugh of all was with the legend Chris Kamara.

Perry Gronstra set a new outright lap record of 50.1 seconds on a 250E kart while wearing a tie under his racing leathers, as he was sponsored by a tie manufacturer. The record stood until Indy 500 winner Takumo Sato bettered it in his Formula 3.

One of the most famous crashes in BTCC history happened at the 1994 event when Gabriele Tarquini was tipped into a multiple roll by Tim Harvey at McIntyre's corner. Murray Walker, the then BTCC commentator was off the scale, and it became one of the most shared BTCC images of all time. Gabriele later returned for a David Leslie tribute meeting and recalled it was the best exposure that Alfa Romeo had ever had!

An annual gathering of Minis of all ages provided an extra attraction at SMRC events when the Mini Coopers were racing. Here, around one hundred Minis take to the track!

A special day to remember Scottish racing legend David Leslie was held on 13 April 2013 when tribute was paid to the Le Mans and British Touring Car winner by all on site with several of his cars, and family, in attendance.

In June 2013, a special anniversary tribute was held for Steve Hislop when his bend was named "Hislop's", with many of his family members present. Every year since Margaret Hislop (below) has presented the Steve Hislop "Flying Haggis" trophy to the rider who sets the fastest race lap, here presenting to Yukio Kagayama.

Chapter 14: Did You Know?   213

In May 2015, to celebrate the 20th anniversary of Colin McRae winning the World Rally Championship, the first McRae Rally Challenge was held in. A host of rally champions was present, including World Champions Hannu Mikkola and Stig Blomqvist, with Jimmy McRae acting as course car. The event was won by Alister McRae in a Proton. In 2022, the second McRae Rally Challenge saw three generations of the McRaes rally head-to-head with grandfather Jimmy, son Alister and grandson Max battling for family honours. The event was attended by multiple world champions including Luis Moya, Louise Aitken Walker, Derek Ringer and Tina Thorner, as well as other stars such as Gwyndaf Evans, Jonny Milner, former bike racer John Crawford and British and European rallycross driver Andy Scott. It was Borders rising star Garry Pearson, with co-driver Ross Kirk, in a Ford Fiesta Rally 2, who took the top honours for the event, just edging out Scott, who had Laura Connell as his navigator. As for the battle of the three generations of the McRaes, it was young Max who won the family honours, finishing seventh overall.

Porsche Germany chose Scotland to celebrate the one millionth Porsche 911, with a tour departing from Edinburgh Castle and finishing with a track day at Knockhill. The first 911, and the millionth, together with every 911 variant from the Porsche Museum in Stuttgart, were on track on 23 May 2017 with journalists from around the world in attendance to capture the extraordinary spectacle.

There have been three 24 hour cycling events at Knockhill for individual and team entrants. The furthest covered by a solo rider is a remarkable 255 miles, almost the same distance from Knockhill to Silverstone! Here Mark Beaumont (centre) poses in the pit lane having established a cycling lap record of 3 minutes flat!

Sir Chris Hoy, Britain's most decorated Olympian, made his rally debut at the McRae Rally Challenge in July 2022 driving a Mitsubishi Evo. Chris is a highly experienced car racer, has competed at Le Mans and is a long-time friend of the McRaes and admirer of Colin, having made a highly rated documentary about him and being allowed to drive the world-famous L555 BAT as part of the programme.

The Forth Road Bridge was also the venue for a British Touring Car/FIA road safety promotion in conjunction with Road Safety Scotland. A collection of Touring Cars was assembled on the south side and driven across the famous Forth Road Bridge on 2 July 2015.

Chapter 14: Did You Know?

To date, the biggest commercial booking for Knockhill was the world launch of the Porsche Cayman GT4. For sixteen days, journalists from around the world were flown in to be welcomed by Porsche's two brand ambassadors, Walter Rhorl and Mark Webber (right).

The circuit at Knockhill has been resurfaced three times in its history. The first happened just prior to the arrival of the BTCC in 1992.

Damon Hill officially opened the Garry Stagg Commentary Tower while visiting to watch his son Josh race in the National Formula Fords.

Knockhill is the venue for a multi-award-winning obstacle course race which includes almost 1000 participants annually. The MacTuff OCR race has been held on the first Sunday in January every year since 2016 (apart from the Covid-19 years). It has won awards for the best organised, most challenging and most original obstacle race, using the fleet of Knockhill Rally cars.

In 2006, the Knockhill team worked with Edinburgh Council to mark the 50th anniversary of the SMRC and Ecurie Ecosse winning the Le Mans 24-hour race. This resulted in Princes Street being closed from the bottom of the Mound to King's Stables Road, allowing a parade of Formula 1 cars, Le Mans cars, British Touring cars and classic race support buses to be driven along the street, to preview the first Scottish Classic SpeedFair Parade.

Part of the circuit, Hislop's, was once the route of a colliery railway line and was originally called Embankment (bend), which led on to Railway Straight, on the run up to Taylor's Turn hairpin.

The Garry Stagg Commentary Tower was named after long-time Knockhill lead commentator Garry Stagg, who pioneered Radio Knockhill 1602MW and subsequently 89.7FM. During his long association with Knockhill, many ground-breaking broadcasts were achieved, including a remarkable live ground-to-pilot broadcast to two Tornado pilots as they did a flypast at speeds of 600mph. The leading car race commentator Robert Johnston was honoured with a presentation by John Cleland at the BTCC event on 30 August 2020.

Kinnaird's Bistro was originally used as the track marshals' canteen, and the toilet block next to it was a jet wash bay.

Double World Superbike Champion and Moto GP rider James Toseland scored his first race win at Knockhill aged just sixteen.

Chapter 14: Did You Know?   217

Possibly the strangest lap record belongs to "Cobblers the Clown" who lapped in 15 minutes 52 seconds on his motorised couch!

TV comedian and presenter Fred MacAulay and TV celebrity chef Nick Nairn were selected as guest drivers for the Ford Credit Fiesta Challenge races supporting the British Touring Cars – and both men acquitted themselves well as they had come to Knockhill for multiple training sessions ahead of their respective events.

Four-times Indy Car Champion Dario Franchitti, GT star Marino Franchitti, Le Mans winner Jonny Adam and multiple BTCC champions Colin Turkington and Gordon Shedden were all regular instructors at the Knockhill Racing Drivers School.

Knockhill hosted Wednesday night Summer Stock Cars on the "oval" with Formula 2s, Hot Rods, Saloons and Mini Stocks. These were hugely popular with the drivers and there were no walls to hit, unlike at Cowdenbeath. The biggest stock car event was a double header visit to Knockhill and Cowdenbeath by the BRISCA Formula 1 stock cars – racing at Knockhill on a Saturday night (in the middle of a British GT meeting!), and then at Cowdenbeath the following afternoon.

Colin McRae was a very regular visitor to his home circuit and filmed part of his DVD "Colin at Play" as he drove his Mk2 Escort, Suzuki Superbike, his development R4 rally car, a Legends race car and numerous other race and rally cars at Knockhill.

Heather Calder from Inverness holds the British Sprint flying lap records of 41.88 seconds clockwise and 42.94 seconds anti-clockwise in her Gould V8 single seater.

Rory Butcher made his British Touring Car debut mid-season at Knockhill in a Shredded Wheat Ford Focus on 12 August 2017. He went on to win his first Knockhill race on 20 August 2019 while driving a Honda Civic.

Moto GP rider Mick Doohan visited Knockhill in 2021 to oversee his son Jack race in the British F4 Championship, while turning the clock back, double Moto GP Champion Casey Stoner raced at Knockhill.

Derek Butcher did a Victor Kiam, as he raced at the very first event in September 1974 and ended up purchasing the circuit some ten years later. Having started on bikes in the 1970s, he then raced cars in the later 1980s, returning to bikes, before competing in Super Lap Scotland in 2023 in his favourite Audi TT.

Part of the circuit, Hislop's, was once a colliery railway line and was originally called Railway Embankment.

As part of their UK tour in 2003, legendary rockers Status Quo played to a capacity crowd of 10,000 on a balmy, still summer's evening on a 100-foot stage built for the occasion at the west end of Paddock 2. The concert featured multiple local bands in support, including Edinburgh-born Fish, of Marillion fame.

Chapter 14: Did You Know?

Knockhill had its first Royal visitor, Prince William, on 22 May 2021. The circuit was hosting a press event for Extreme E, used in the all-electric rally championship, and Prince William, now the Prince of Wales, drove the ProDrive prepared car and learned about their hydrogen-fuelled generators. The Knockhill team are pleased to have met, and chatted with Prince William. Here, left to right, Gemma Hobbs (Events Manager), Alan Brunton (Operations Manager), Stuart Gray (Director of Events), Prince William, Jillian Shedden (Managing Director) and Gordon Shedden (Business Development Manager) share some time together after William's drive.

The "Wullie Brown Marshals Building" is named after a much-missed Knockhill staff member who sadly passed away at only fifty years old. Wullie was the Chief Track Marshal and is much missed. The KMSC present the Wullie Brown Trophy in his memory at every event they run, for the Spirit of the Meeting award.

There used to be a paintball fort in the middle of the circuit, which was operated by the then operators of the Karting Centre with paintball war games even going on while the track was live!

The British Superbikes and Knockhill took over George Square, Glasgow in 2011 and 2012 and one of the highlights was the Go Fast Jet Pack Man, Eric Scott, launching himself off the top of the City Chambers buildings to land in the Square below. Hugely spectacular and entertaining for the thousands of folk below.

Moto 2 rider Rory Skinner was given special KMSC/SACU dispensation to race at the age of eleven. After multiple championship wins, he made his first Knockhill BSB appearance on a Kawasaki on 11 July 2021. He progressed to Moto 2 in 2023, having secured two podiums and the much-coveted Steve Hislop Trophy at the 2022 Knockhill BSB round.

Chart-topping band the Kaiser Chiefs recorded their video for their 2016 song "Hole In My Soul" at Knockhill over three days. They used the fleet of Civic Type Rs, with the Knockhill drivers replacing band members for the driving element of the video.

Knockhill Racing Circuit Limited was awarded the Gold Covenant for services to the armed forces on 13 November 2019.

Chapter 14: Did You Know?

Tracey and Scott Dickson tied the knot at the 2013 British Superbikes event with leading riders lending their support to their wedding day.

For the first twenty years of the venue, the Tri Oval link road was a red blaze surface and early rallycross and stock car events used the mixture of surfaces for their race events.

In the late 1980s, in one of the biggest televised events, the annual Scottish Super Prix was a showcase, non-championship race event that featured drivers such as Damon Hill, Martin Donnelly, David and Gary Brabham, Scott Stringfellow and many other young aspiring Formula 1 drivers. The 1987 event ended prematurely for Damon Hill who sensationally crashed at Duffus Dip, 300 metres after the start, after testing all week long.

There have been many Formula 1 car demos at Knockhill including Sir Jackie Stewart's Tyrrell and James Hunt's Marlboro McLaren, but the only time a contemporary Formula 1 car appeared was the sensational ex-Schumacher/Barichello Ferrari in 2006. The V10 screamer was driven by Aberdonian Nathan Kinch to a lap time of 40.3 seconds, becoming the fastest-ever vehicle to lap Knockhill. On the same day at the MotorFair, he drove a Ferrari FXX, one of only twenty-seven ever produced.

Westminster Cabinet Ministers Lord Mandelson and Geoff Hoon hosted a major media and press conference on the future of motoring and energy production at Knockhill. It featured the world's first all-electric pre-production BMW Mini, which was brought from Germany under conditions of considerable secrecy by their head of development in 2010.

The latest addition to the karting Centre is the purchase of a two-seater kart so that adults can take their child as young four years old and upwards. Here Knockhill Sales Manager Laura Graham takes daughter Jorja for a thrill run, or is it the other way round?

One of the newest events to be created by the events team is the Live Action Family Fireworks event every November. This has rapidly become a fans favourite and has is now the third largest event of the calendar.

1n 1995, Audi Sport recorded the highest ever track temperature of over 50 degrees celsius, at that time, by their BTCC race team with Frank Biela and John Bintcliffe.

Chapter 14: Did You Know?

The largest gathering of sidecars was brought together at the 2023 KMSC-organised Jock Taylor Trophy event on 2 and 3 September. Over sixty sidecars were on track for a parade and photo shoot with guests of honour Steve Webster MBE (ten-time World Sidecar Champion) and Paul Woodhead (left) with Jock Talylor's niece, Yvonne Taylor, on board Jock's world championship winning sidecar (right).

Knockhill became one of the first locations in Scotland to have an electric car charging station. This was following a media event by the then Scottish Minister of Transport, Keith Brown, who rolled out a Scottish Government-funded provision of 250 charging points across Scotland in 2012.

Opposite: A dramatic "off" captured by Alex Ireland as a rider exits stage left at McIntyre's and slides across the gravel trap.

Chapter 15
Fan's Favourites

A Selection of Highlights

Top left: James Samsun captures a high-flying Gordon Shedden as he launches off the Duffus Dip kerb.

Top right: Two stars together: Jet Pack Man goes for a flight as stunt driver Terry Grant climbs on board his spinning Legend

Second row, left: Jim Maguire captures a smiling Bradley Ray.

Third row, left: One of the early customers in the Tom Brown Racing School in 1982 was Ian Cochrane who enjoyed his run in the Van Dieman Formula Ford 1600.

Above: If Carlsberg did Bike Track Day instructors, they would be at Knockhill! Here Sean Garswood has an instructor lineup of John MacGuinness and Niall Mackenzie.

Bottom left: Getting the knee and elbow down! Rory Skinner is captured by Neil Smith at an incredible angle.

Left: Legends racing has seen a real growth in popularity recently with grids in the mid-20s and were a hit at the 2023 Touring Cars event too. These popular motorcycle engined racers are also used within Knockhill's Driving Experiences. Here Duncan Vincent (7) tries a manoeuvre on race leader David Hunter (6).

Bottom left: A great photo sent in by Mhairi LIgertwood of her father George who loved bikes and rode and worked with bikes most of his life.

Above: Keith Chegwin in the driving seat of a Challenger tank – what could possibly go wrong? Oops, something just has, as he crushes a parked car at the 2006 Scottish MotorFair.

Below: Derek Horne sent in this close-up of Sam Munro as he rounds the Taylor's Turn hairpin.

Chapter 15: Fan's Favourites   227

Top: Alex Ireland captures a candid shot of Damon Hill and his son Josh discussing tactics before a National Formula Ford race. Unfortunately, Josh was to get a puncture while leading.

Middle left: Blair McConachie sent in this one of himself as he had huge success at his home track when the Caterham Championships came north for a Twin Track weekend.

Middle right: Track marshals Garry Stevenson and Jamie Nicolson pose in the pitlane at the end of the 2022 car race season.

Bottom: Up, up and away! A scary "off" for Bailey Stuart Campbell at the hairpin!

Opposite: Without marshals there would be no racing! The car and bike marshals provide an invaluable role to keep any race day going safely as they communicate with competitors through the use of flags and lights, go to their rescue in the event of an incident, communicate with Race Control about any issues on track, put out the occasional fire and help keep the track in tip-top condition too. Marshals – we salute you all!

Chapter 15: Fan's Favourites

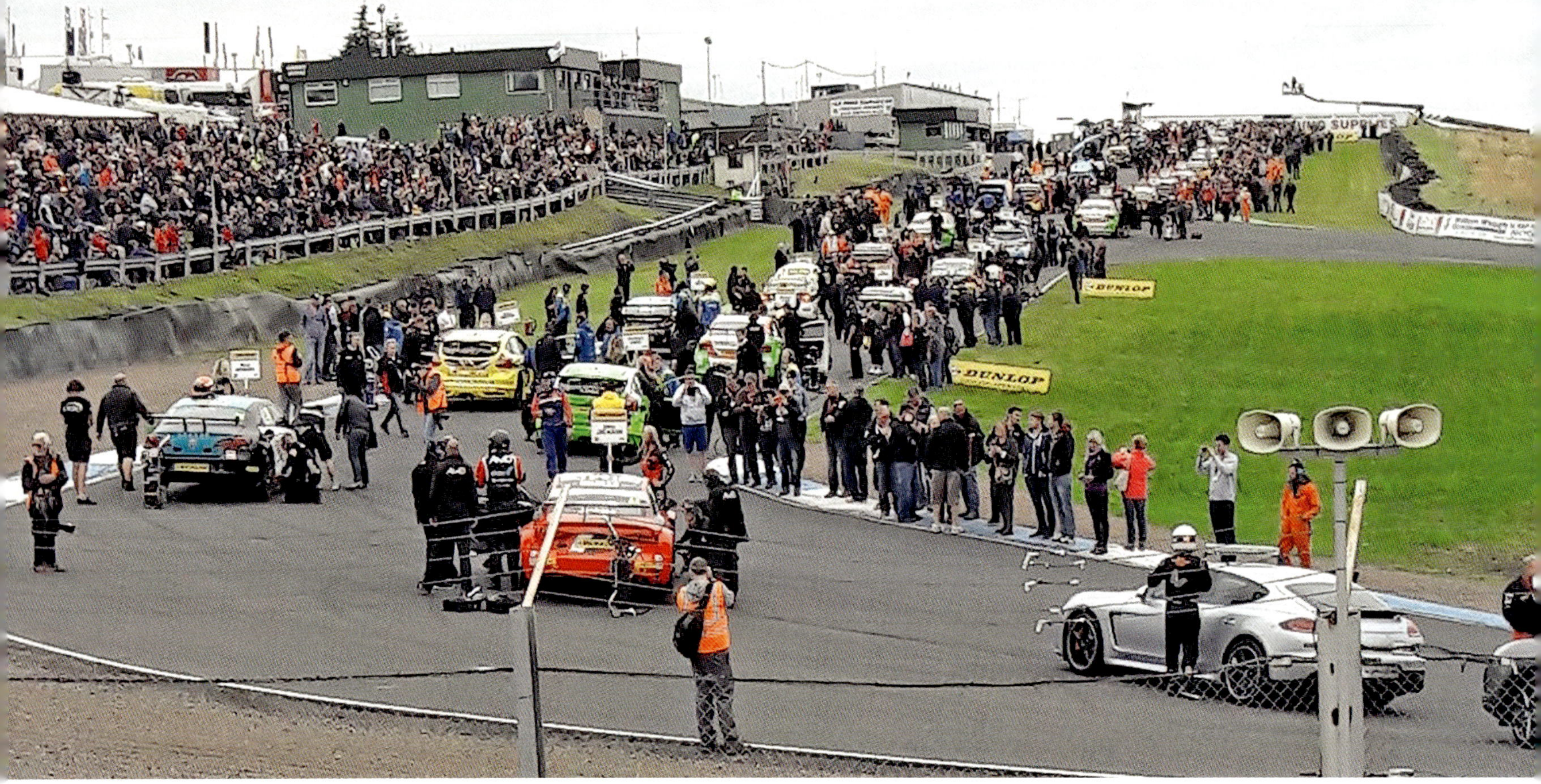
DUNLOP
DUNLOP

LEXELLE.COM
amtech
www.ktm4u.co.uk
redline
95
MOTOREX

BTCC

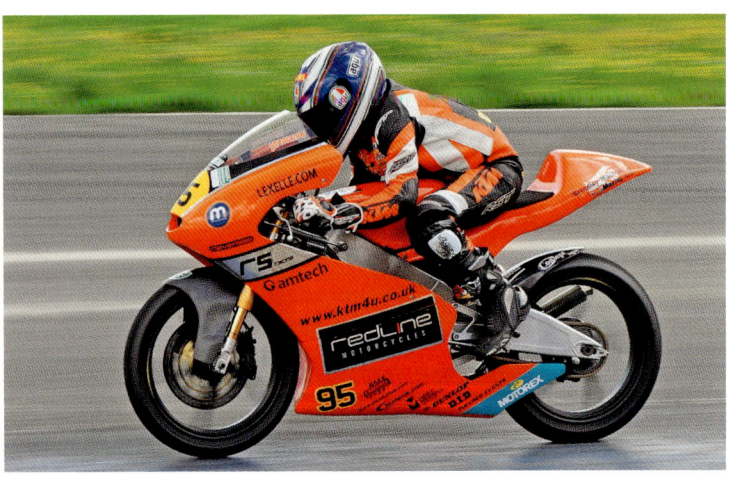

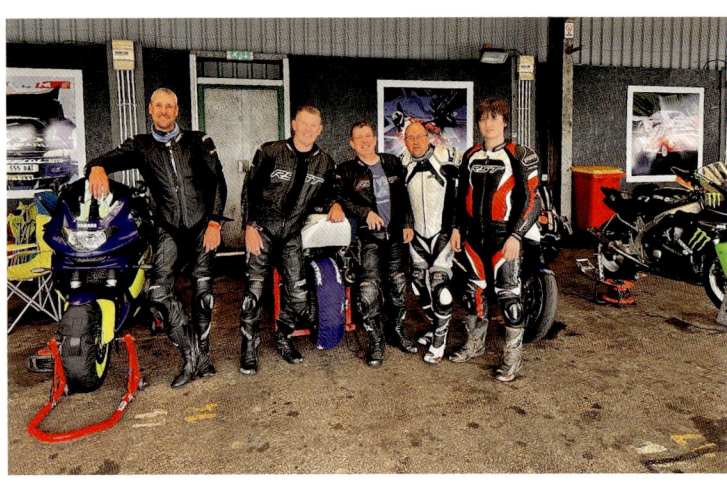

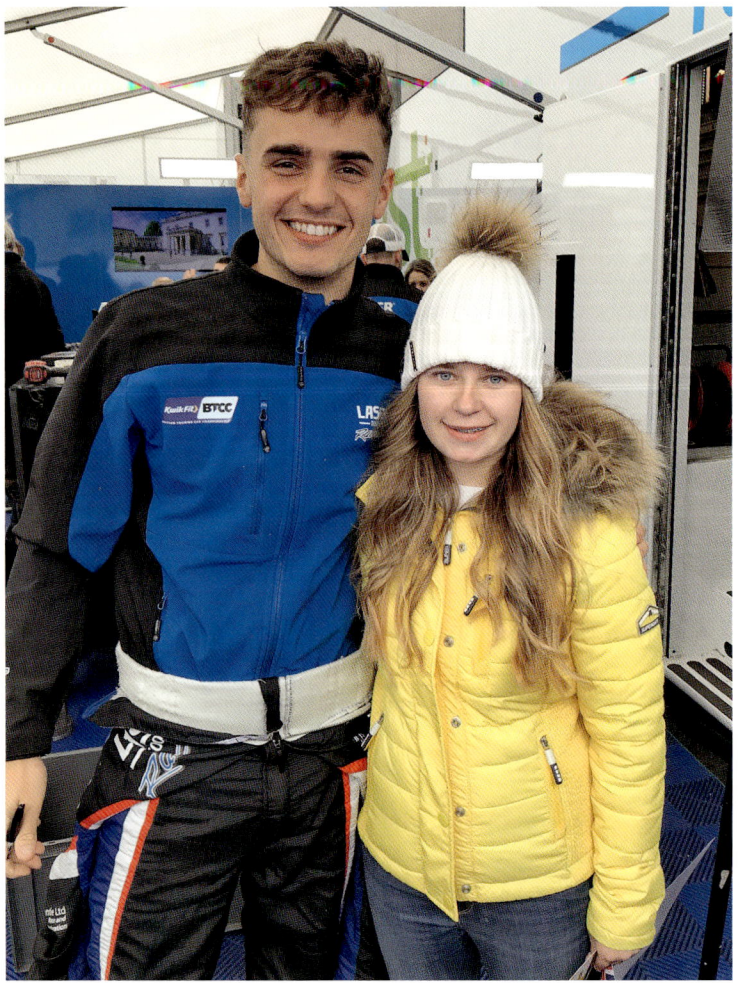

Opposite, top: A packed grid of 32 Touring Cars stretches all the way to the hairpin providing spectators a great view of a mass start – and what a noise too!

Opposite, centre: Alex Griffin took this picture of a very young Tarran Mackenzie in 2012.

Opposite, bottom left: Track day fun at the Niall Mackenzie Superbikes Experience! .

Opposite, bottom right: Shana Cheyne catches up with her favourite driver, BTCC racer Aiden Moffat.

Left: Sir Jackie Stewart was reunited with one of his Tyrrell Formula 1 cars, much to the delight of a big crowd at the first Scottish Classic SpeedFair.

Below: The Scottish Motor Marshals show off their latest response vehicles including the dedicated Forexo Fire One vehicle (left).

Chapter 15: Fan's Favourites   231

Below: The original commentary box dating back to the mid 1970s, resembled more of a sentry box. It provided an excellent panoramic view of most of the circuit.

Opposite: Damon Hill was called upon to open the newly raised and extended commentary tower, and the full team that year gladly joined in the ribbon cutting ceremony. Pictured here from left to right are Joe Tanner, Robert Johnston, Gylen Boardman, Damon Hill, Duncan Vincent, a proud Garry Stagg, and Dennis Hobbs.

Chapter 16
Tales from the Tower

Commentary Team Highlights

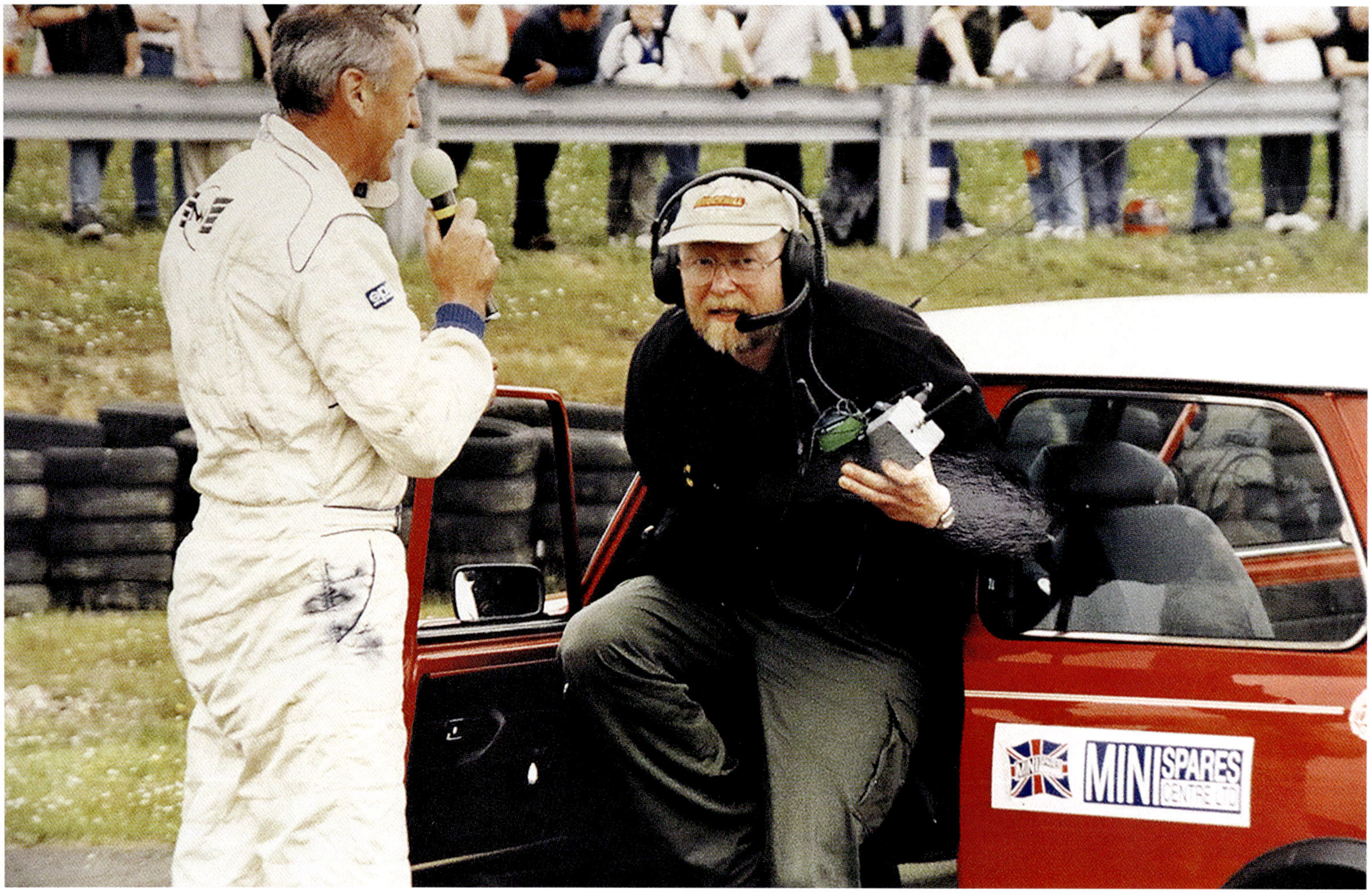
MINI SPARES
CENTRE LTD

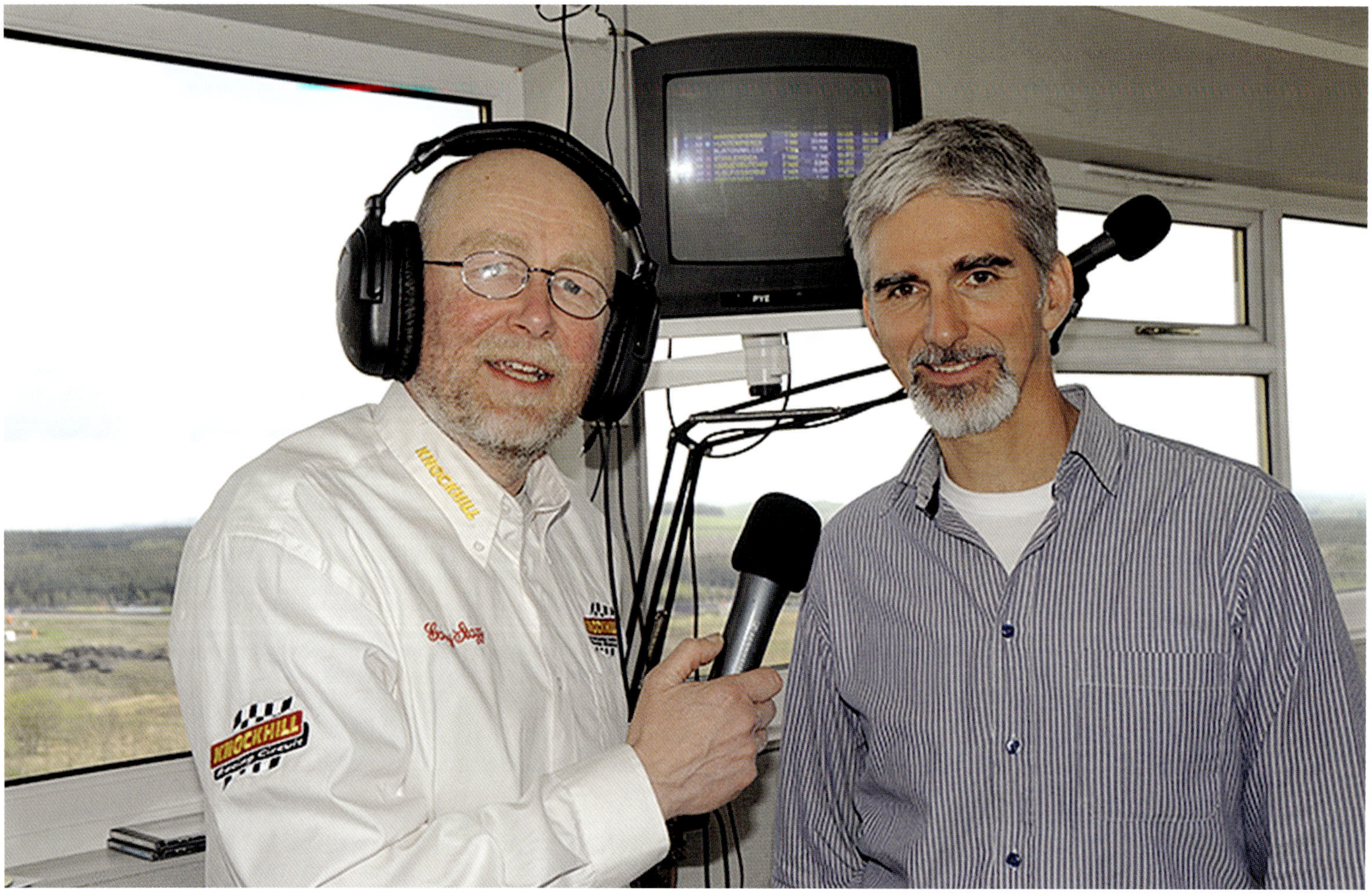
KNOCKHILL

This is the story of how Knockhill has developed the UK's best and most innovative commentary service and commentary team to rival any circuit in Europe.

There have been three commentators who have stood the test of time at Knockhill. Garry Stagg, the longest serving so far, has had to retire – mostly owing to injuries sustained in a motorcycle accident. With over twenty-five years' service, Robert Johnston – aka the Doc – is still to be heard at every SMRC and BTCC race meeting. Duncan Vincent remains a Knockhill regular and dovetails his core work at Knockhill with national British Superbike and international championships – yet another first-class Scottish export.

Here, in their own words, they relate some of what has made Knockhill a very special part of their lives and careers.

Opposite, top: Going for a spin! Garry emerges from Russ Swift's Mini Cooper having experienced on of his amazing stunt displays.

Opposite, bottom: A proud day! Garry meets an icon, Damon Hill, and had a chance to interview him at length during the opening of the new commentary tower.

Garry Stagg's Commentary Recollections

If truth be told, becoming involved with motorsports commentary was almost an accident. Certainly, I would watch Grands Prix on TV and was even daft enough to fantasise that maybe I could do that. Perhaps not Murray Walker, but still . . . My first love was always motorcycling and at least I had the wit to realise that I had neither the talent nor the courage to take it up competitively. My enthusiasm for racing involved spectating at East Fortune, Silloth, the TT and, of course, Knockhill.

However, one day at a race meeting, my wife Hilda spotted an advert in a Knockhill programme seeking a commentator. You see, it was her idea – honest! The full training mentioned in the advert consisted of being handed a microphone and told to "talk into this end". Actually, that was the only thing that I did know about. Somehow, thirty years later, I was still doing it.

Mostly, I was terrified, convinced that everyone around knew far more about this sport than I did (that, at least, was probably true). Nevertheless, excitement, enthusiasm and simple fear carried me through. In those early days, timekeeping was carried out by lap scorers and a primitive computer in Race Control, linked to an optical timing beam at the start/finish line. There was absolutely no communication with the tower. I was equipped only with a pair of binoculars, that microphone and a programme. At my side was the late Ian Robertson, whose first and possibly only love was motorcycle sport. He gave all his spare time and a substantial proportion of his wages in sponsorship and support to up-and-coming riders. He would regale me with a constant stream of facts and background information – which was really helpful, although occasionally he offered a slightly original interpretation. Through my own business I had access to professional audio equipment. I was pleased to use this if it would augment the surprisingly good public address system – surprising because, at club level, somewhat dismal kit was usually the norm. The fact was that Derek had no hesitation in acquiring new equipment if it improved the spectator experience.

Apart from a policy of continual maintenance and upgrades to the PA system, the most significant advance was Radio Knockhill – later Knockhill FM. This came about because when Derek had been to Le Mans for the 24-hour race he had been impressed by the English-language radio commentary service. Being aware of my involvement with local community radio, he asked if something similar could be achieved at Knockhill. With all the confidence of the blissfully ignorant, bolstered by the knowledge that I could call upon well-qualified contacts who would hopefully keep me out of too much trouble, I happily assured him that it would be a doddle. Little did I realise how many sleepless nights were coming up. Plans, projections and costings were presented to Derek. A medium wave transmitter had to be acquired, which was likely to be so costly that the project might never happen. Fortunately, I knew an individual who, like me, had more enthusiasm than sense. He was able to manufacture a suitable low-power device at an affordable price. It was based on a 1950s military design using – would you believe? – valves. Built like the proverbial brick outhouse it served us well for over twenty years – they don't make 'em like that anymore.

Sports stadium radio services are common nowadays, but in 1992 they were unknown. At that time the regulatory body was the Radio Authority (later to be Ofcom). They could issue a Restricted Service Licence. Intended to permit small-scale broadcasts for specific events – for example, an arts festival – would it allow us to broadcast for a whole season? Transmissions were allowed for twenty-eight days and these would have to include transmitter testing. Carefully reading the guidance notes for applicants for RSLs, we realised that the twenty-eight days could be spread over seven months. This sort of thing had not actually been done before, so Knockhill would be a UK first. We could do it – the question was, were the powers-that-be going to allow it?

A carefully worded application was duly completed and sent in with the (quite substantial) non-refundable deposit. It would take six weeks to get approval for an RSL. Should we gamble and order the specialist equipment we would need? If we wanted to be on air in time for Scotland's first ever British Touring Car Championship meeting, we had to do it. For the

Left: The Master and The Apprentice! Duncan Vincent (the apprentice) showing Garry Stagg (the master) the way to go.

next six weeks, I could hardly think of anything else. Then one day the phone rang, and it was Jillian to tell me that the license had been approved. It is worth noting that the team at the radio authority had been helpful and friendly throughout.

During the weeks prior to BTCC, a few all-nighters were pulled as studio equipment was installed and commissioned. Then Trefor – a Welshman from Sheffield – arrived with the transmitter. Everything was connected and a test tone generated. That very moment, there was a loud click followed by an ominous silence. By one of those incredible twists of coincidence an arc welder on the far side of the track had been activated at the exact split-second when we switched on. The resulting power spike took out a vital part of the transmitter chain. The nearest spare part was over 300 miles away – a sticky moment: was this all falling apart? Trefor drove all night to get two (one and a spare). Oh, yes, and a whacking great surge protector – no more schoolboy errors, please! The next time we switched on, everything worked as it should and a valuable lesson had been learned, just in time.

The touring cars arrived and a small town grew in the paddocks. Bob Dawson, a prince among engineers, was on hand to coordinate the commentary requirements of BTCC with the circuit facilities. He freely gave of his time, his experience and his technical knowledge. We all held our breath and full-time trackside motorsport radio commentary in Great Britain was born in Scotland.

As the seasons passed, more technical progress was made. Some pretty creative use of antenna networks meant that we were able to offer live in-car commentary. Bearing in mind that the sort of equipment used for motorsport on TV often costs north of £10,000 per system, we were fortunate to be able to tailor more modest equipment to our needs. We also managed to provide reliable radio mics for pit lane commentary and post-race interviews. When Duncan Vincent joined the commentary team, he would regularly test the equipment's limits. He had an uncanny ability to be where the action was and to make live on-air contributions, no matter how obscure the location.

There were problems of course. When we installed the system in a Formula Ford the vibrations shook out every single nut, bolt and screw in the damn thing. When BTCC used their mobile podium, it was scheduled to stop exactly opposite the main race day sponsors enclosure for some live interviews with drivers. Sadly, this proved to be the very location where a radio microphone simply could not work – five metres to either side would have been fine. Mineral deposits under the ground will do that to you. However, both BSB and BTCC commentators have remarked that Knockhill was the only circuit in Great Britain where the radio mic could be relied upon absolutely. High praise indeed!

The day came when, finally, the old MW transmitter had to go. I had spent the entire Sunday of a BTCC meeting managing the studio side of commentary for Ian Titchmarsh. There might have been a little stress here. I was acutely aware that my friend and colleague Martin Hobson was standing downstairs quite literally holding bits of wire together to keep the transmitter alive. For us, however, the main thing was that the broadcast continued and that spectators were wholly unaware that anything was amiss. The decision was made that in future we would be an FM station. A new transmitter was ordered and installed, steam radio was retired, and greater clarity came to the airwaves around Knockhill.

One of the most spectacular moments and a technical achievement of which we could be very proud was when the RAF came to visit. This was to be a fly-past at the start of the main feature Touring Car race. Could we manage to get this on-air? We knew that the event would be coordinated between RAF Leuchars and Race Control. The RAF were kind enough to let us know the visiting aircrafts' cockpit frequency. Martin once more came to the rescue. A technical genius and good friend to the circuit, he was able to loan us a scanner that could receive this, while I was able to scrounge a remarkably complex-looking antenna array. Everything was hooked up and plugged in to the broadcast and PA systems.

There had been no possibility of a rehearsal, so we had absolutely no idea if this was going to work. At the appropriate time the word came to stand by and I started monitoring the radio frequency. I could hear the pilots speaking to one another as they were stooging around above the Wallace Monument near Stirling. Meanwhile, the cars had completed their green flag lap and were lined up on the starting grid. We warned spectators that the situation was about to become extremely noisy and that ear protection, especially for the very young, was highly advisable. What was actually about to happen, however, was not revealed. As the aircraft started their approach, the advice was to look west.

Left: A proud day for the Knockhill team with the naming of the tower, the Garry Stagg Commentary Tower. Owner Derek Butcher, managing director Jillian Shedden, lead commentator Duncan Vincent and director of events, Stuart Gray mark the occasion.

Above: Garry and Hilda Stagg still enjoy regular visits to either the Superbikes or Touring Cars. Behind Garry is the Garry Stagg Commentary Tower which is named in his honour and for services to broadcasting at Knockhill.

Two tiny black dots appeared in the sky above Bridge of Allan. As they grew larger the channel volume for the cockpit radios was turned up. "65 Squadron Attack! Attack! Attack!" The two dots became two RAF Tornadoes that appeared to brush the chimney tops of the nearby farmhouse then swooped in low over the hairpin and along the main straight. As they got to the footbridge they pulled into a vertical climb, lit the afterburners and went ballistic into the sky. The red lights on the bridge went out, the race started and every alarm in the car park was activated! Meanwhile, the voice from above: "65 Squadron returning to Leuchars, thank you very much, Knockhill." The channel was closed and Ian Titchmarsh began to commentate the race. The technical team heaved a huge sigh of relief – we had done our bit and everything worked!

Three Scary Moments

- Exiting the hairpin while commentating as a passenger on a sidecar demonstration lap and wondering if my fingers were going to let me hang on: then arriving seconds later under the bridge and wishing I had let go at the hairpin because it would have hurt a lot less if I did it then at 30mph than if I did it now at 130mph!
- Trying to commentate from the pillion seat of official Triumph stunt rider Kevin Carmichael's bike as he rode up the main straight at 100mph on one wheel.
- Interviewing "Jet Pack Man" on top of the Glasgow City Council buildings when he stepped off and flew around George Square at a "Superbikes in the Square" promotion.

My Scariest Moment

- Wearing a hard hat, leaning on a ladder at the top of the yet to be completed new commentary tower. It was the first bike race meeting of the season, the builders' schedule had been hit by the weather and I was attempting to commentate in what felt like the open air in a howling gale through a cobbled-together excuse for a PA system.

Four Exhilarating Moments

- Commentating as a passenger in cars including a European Rallycross Championship-winning Sierra RS500, two different Ferraris, numerous racing cars, on two wheels in Russ Swift's Austin Montego.
- Commentating as a "human bollard" at an autocross demonstration by Willie Greig.
- Having my toes run over by Terry Grant in his TVR.
- Lapping the circuit in a kit car driven by Sir Jack Brabham.

All in all, it has been a great privilege to have had the opportunity to be part of the development of Scotland's Motorsport Centre and to have witnessed so much from the inside. Being around for more than half of the first fifty years has been an amazing experience. The next fifty years will see enormous changes. It is good to know that whatever the future holds for motorsport in Scotland, Knockhill is in very good hands.

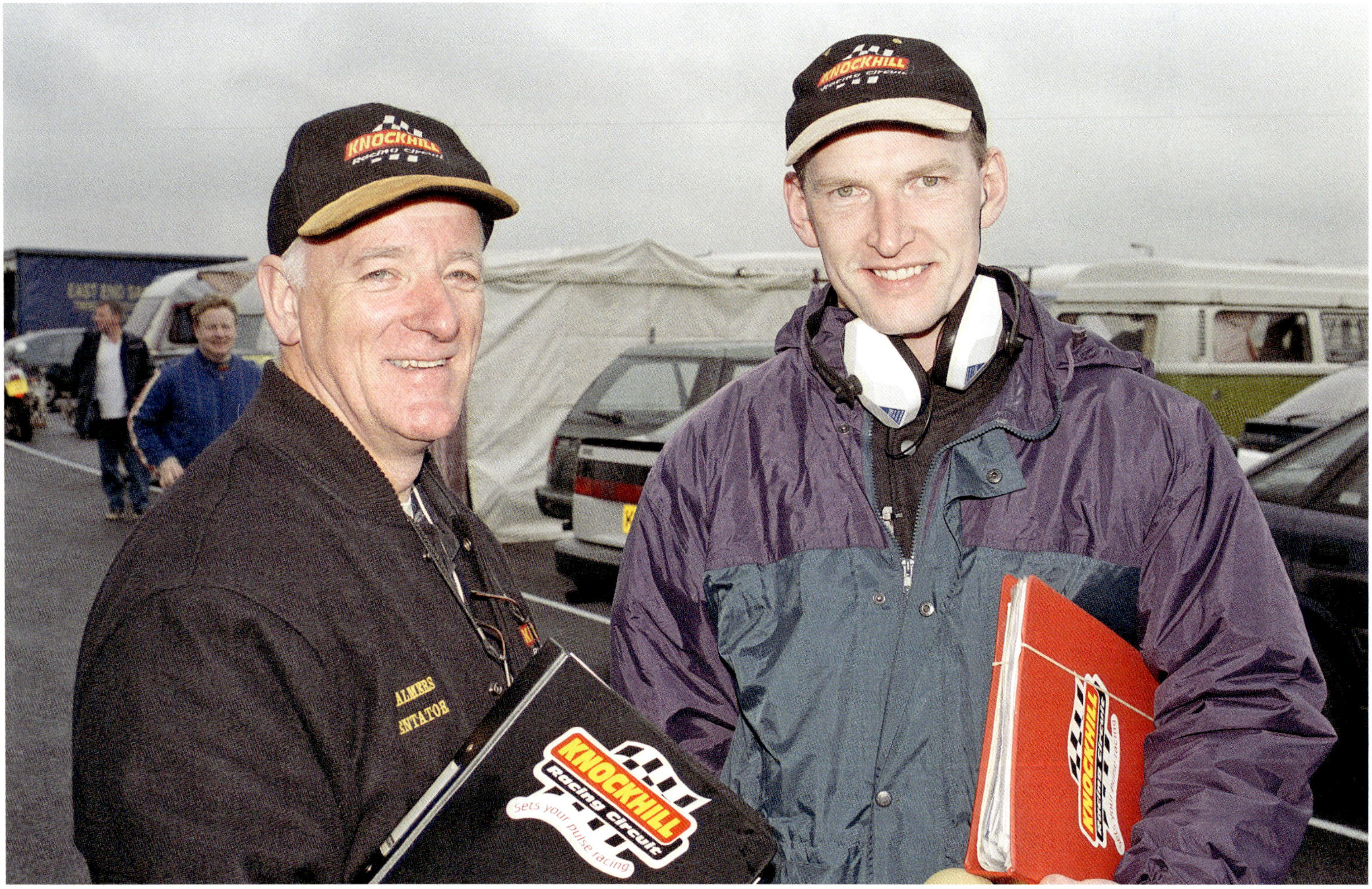

238 Knockhill: 50 Years of Racing

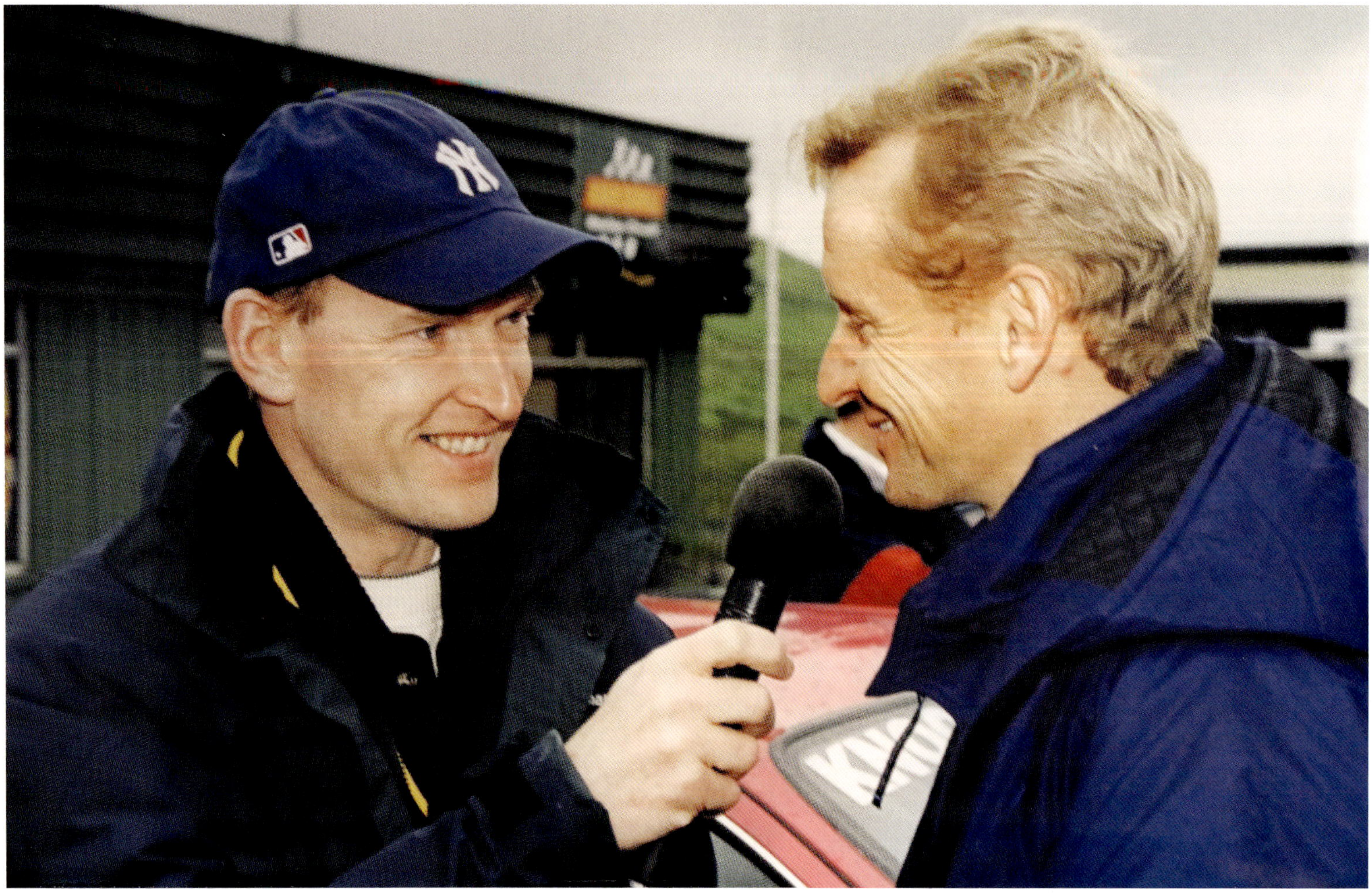

> **One of the great benefits of being a commentator is the access to drivers and teams. You get to meet your heroes.**

Opposite, top: A regular at all car events was John Chalmers (left). John loved car racing and his knowledge of the sport was exceptional. He's seen here pictured with "Doc" Robert Johnston.

Opposite, bottom: One of Robert's favourite Interviewees was Texan Kevin Shwartz who was one of the easiest to chat with, even though Robert mainly specialised in car sport.

Robert Johnston's Commentary Recollections

My start in commentary came from a conversation with Stuart Gray in late 1995, which ended with the classic, "If you think you can do better, then come and have a go." So in early 1996 I started as pit lane commentator with John Chalmers as lead commentator.

The old commentary box was about ten feet lower than today's tower and much smaller. It was crammed with Garry Stagg's broadcasting and PA system, no timing computers, no instant result print-outs, no internet. But we had Garry. Very subtly he provided fantastic training for me, and I didn't ever realise he was training me. The lessons learned in those early days with Garry have lasted forever.

Then Duncan Vincent arrived. I'd met Duncan a few times through his XR2 racing. His commentary debut, with me now leading the race commentary in the tower and Duncan covering pit lane, paddock and hairpin, was epic. That famous line, "You're on live radio, don't say cock or bugger" had Garry and me in stitches. Seeing Duncan evolve into the best circuit commentator in the UK and develop a superb ability in podcast and video presentation has been one of the most rewarding aspects of my commentary career. It's always a great experience when we get the chance to work together; there's a chemistry that just seems to work on air. It's also down to Duncan that so many people know me as "the Doc". Something to do with the Beatles song "Doctor Robert" I think. Coming up to date, we now have a really strong commentary team who can all work very well together and talk from genuine experience in motorsport.

Random Great Moments!

Are you a real doctor? No I'm not, but thanks to Duncan christening me as Doctor Robert, there are always people who are confused. John Marshall once asked me, just after a podium presentation, if I could check his stitches from some recent surgery. He really shouldn't have been racing that day, but he had a championship to win. More recently, after we all returned to racing action after Covid-19, someone asked me if I was still busy treating Covid-19 patients. I've also been named in race programmes and in even in *Autosport* magazine as Dr Robert. Funny how these things stick.

The loose wheel and my Murray Walker moment. It was my second or third ever commentary appearance in 1996. John Muir had a hugely powerful and highly modified Toyota Starlet competing in the SMRC modified Sports and Saloon car championship. An archrival was Barclay Dougall with his Ford Sierra RS500. Barclay had been plagued with reliability issues but in this race he was heading for the podium in second place. I was commentating from the pit lane, and as Barclay came past to start his last lap, I said, "Barclay looking safe now in a good second place as he starts his last lap." And at that very moment his front left wheel came off, right in front of me. The classic curse of the commentator.

Damon and the blues. One of the great benefits of being a commentator is the access to drivers and teams. You get to meet your heroes. I remember a warm sunny day chatting to Damon Hill and his wife Georgie about the great blues guitarist, Robert Johnson. I was waiting to go on air for a lunchtime interview with Damon, and as great music lover, he recognised my name. Not quite my spelling, but it sounds the same as the blues maestro.

That Jason Plato thing. I have several Jason Plato autographs, but I like the story behind the last one I got. This was written on the opening page of my copy of his book *How Not to Become a Professional Racing Driver*. He wrote, "To Robert, thanks for the editorial balance, Jason Plato." At BTCC meetings there is always great support for Gordon Shedden and he deservedly gets a lot of air time along with the other Scottish drivers. I'm also a Shedden fan, but to provide a balance on air, I chose to be the Plato fan in the house. It made for some great on-air banter with Duncan and the team over several years of BTCC coverage. At Jason's last BTCC event at Knockhill in 2022, Duncan set up an interview with Jason and Matt Neal. It made for compelling viewing on YouTube, but it was the hour of chat beforehand, mostly un-broadcastable, that was truly memorable.

Above: Guest commentators often visit the Garry Stagg Tower. Here, Tim Harvey and Paul O'Neil share a laugh.

Opposite: A star in the making! The antics and car control of Harry King are becoming legendary as he continues his meteoric rise in the sports car world.

BTCC. It's been a great honour for Duncan and me to have commentated at the BTCC rounds at Knockhill since 2015. A high standard is expected and we both work hard on the preparation for that one. In 2015 we had about two days' notice that we were on, but since then we've known well in advance, luckily. It's a real buzz to look out from the commentary tower and see the circuit lined with fans right around the full lap. There was also the 2020 event where Alan Hyde was unable to travel and so I had to take over his pit lane and podium role. Hydie shared some trade secrets with me in advance but it was still a challenge. I loved it.

British GT. "There's half a million pounds worth of Ferraris in the gravel at the chicane" is a line I always remember delivering. I think it was around 2004 or 2005 that we last had British GT at Knockhill. It was a real test of driver skill to thread these extremely fast cars around the twists and turns of Knockhill and there were a few incidents along the way. I remember about a quarter of the way into one of the races one of the Ferraris spun into the gravel at the chicane exit. Two or three laps later another Ferrari landed there. After that we had a red flag to calm things down a bit.

Robin Drysdale and the seagull. Legend cars fly in close formation, so do seagulls. Late one summer afternoon, the Legends set off for their ten-lap final race. A couple of laps into the race, a spectator at the braking point for turn one had had enough of their packed lunch and decided to scatter the remaining food across the trackside grass for the birds to pick up. As several large seagulls tucked into the unexpected

feast, the leading pack of Legends came charging under the bridge around 120mph. The seagulls eventually noticed the approaching cars, but slightly too late. There was a flapping of wings and feathers flying while they attempted their escape, but one of them was just a touch too slow. That became obvious about 30 seconds later when Robin Drysdale accelerated out of Clark's corner and then failed to change up a gear. A split second later a very large seagull was thrown out of the side window of Robin's car and bounced along the trackside. The bird had gone straight through the front screen and jammed against the gear lever. With the bird removed, Robin carried on battling for the race win. "That's the only time you'll see Robin Drysdale throwing a bird out of his car at the weekend" was my summary of the whole thing.

Feeding the commentators. It started with Andrew Howard's Beechdean Dairy Ice Cream GT team. We mentioned Beechdean a few times and amazingly a tray of Beechdean ice cream was delivered. Then there was Steve and Seb Perez and the Amigos Tequila flavoured beer. We mentioned that a couple of times as the relevant car was in the thick of the race action, and a couple of crates of it duly arrived in the box. Then there's Henry Dawes. the Ginetta GT5 driver, moving up to the Porsche Carrera Cup GB for 2023. He has a Domino's Pizza franchise and a Domino's liveried race car. Duncan and I just happened to wonder on air if he could do deliveries to Knockhill. And of course he did, twice. It was wonderful. Finally there is Burnett Motorsport, the Legends race team who regularly deliver a tasty morning fry-up and some cakes to the tower.

Seven unforgettable events

1. 2006 Motorshow event with Scuderia Ecosse Ferraris and Nathan Kinch setting what at the time was the fastest ever Knockhill lap in a Ferrari 2003GA. Duncan's summary: "All that Ferrari Formula 1 technology and they put a guy from Kelty on the refuelling rig."

2. 2006 Classic SpeedFair with Jackie Stewart, Jimmy Stewart, Tyrrell demos, Ecurie Ecosse and more best races ever.

3. Harry King in the Porsche Carrera Cup 2020, coming from near the back of the grid to take the lead on the final lap. I was in the pit garages for the last three laps and the atmosphere was amazing. Everyone knew they were witnessing something special.

4. Turkington vs Sutton, BTCC Race 2 2021

5. Mini Cooper Cup supporting BTCC about 2014 I think. Chris Smiley won, but it was the four wide move into Duffus that was a special moment.

6. Most National Formula Ford races and most Caterham races

7. Best Overtakers: Finlay Mickel – back of the Legends grid to win in 6 laps, overtaking 23 cars in the process Dave Newsham – overtaking 17 cars on the opening lap of a Legends race. Harry King – see the best races section above.

Chapter 16: Tales From the Tower

242 Knockhill: 50 Years of Racing

Opposite, top: "Doc" Robert Johnston is a picture of concentration after being part of the team for over twenty years.

Opposite, bottom: Graeme Bodel has become a regular member of the team during the 2020s. Being an ex-racer himself, he has a vast and specialist knowledge of bike racing.

Below left: They say "never meet your hero", but in this case Duncan made an exception, meeting five-time 500cc World Champion Mick Doohan!

Below right: Always on the move!

Duncan Vincent's Commentary Recollections

For me, commentary started one day when Jillian had to leave Knockhill at lunchtime and a pit lane commentator was required. I was asked if I would like to do it. I was very nervous. It was not something that I had ever thought I could do. Nor was it something that I had really been interested in. I was a racer and I wanted to race. That's all.

Garry Stagg was very much the man behind Radio Knockhill. He was always helpful, supportive and keen for me to be involved with all aspects of commentary. I started with pit lane punditry then Garry encouraged me into the commentary box to expand my skills. We did not just cover motorsport. We would present shows like MotorFair and SpeedFair at Knockhill as well as representing the circuit during events such as the Scottish Bike Show at Ingliston.

Opposite, top: Always work with a smile on your face!

Opposite, bottom: Le Mans winner Allan McNish has been a regular visitor with both Audi and SMRC roles to fulfil. He's always the consummate professional when being interviewed.

Highlights

Damon Hill: Officially oppening the new commentary box.

Mick Doohan: Spending a full weekend in the commentary box watching over his son, Jack.

In-car commentary: We pioneered live commentary from the driver's seat. I even succeeded in winning races as well as qualifying in pole position while talking about it!

Upgrading: Radio Knockhill 1602MW to Knockhill FM.

"Don't say cock or bugger": I blame Alan Brunton and the young ones for this.

BTCC: Being given the opportunity to lead the commentary team after an illness kept Ian Titchmarsh away. A great moment for the Dunc 'n' Doc partnership.

BSB: Being asked to be number two at BSB 2017 and cover the Race 2 grid walk.

Naming the man: Robert Johnston becomes Dr Robert – aka "The Doc".

Stock cars: In at the deep end covering Wednesday evening stock cars after the series commentator's transport broke down on the way to the event.

Talent: Bringing in new talent has given the team strength and a great mixture of knowledge. I'm extremely proud of managing the team so that they communicate with each other at work and personally. They have kept me motivated. I have an inbuilt chemistry with Doc; commentary flows with great ease and we could quite easily finish each other's sentences. We never crash over the top of each other. I see Doc and me as complete equals in the box. There is never an ego or "elbows out I'm in charge" issue. That's the key to how we work so well and have continued together over a long period.

Unusual happenings: Interviewing sidecar competitor David Wrinn when he had a cardiac arrest while speaking on the mic right in front of me. If you are going to have a heart attack, have it at a race circuit – we have got first-aid trained commentators and marshals, doctors, paramedics, defibrillators and ambulances to look after you!

Andrew Gallacher: When he had a massive lead in the race, he was accelerating on the straight and waved to me as I was commentating from the pit wall. I spotted that his fuel line was dragging on the ground. I was able to give him a warning wave and on the next lap he come into the pit lane with fuel pouring from the car. He parked over a drain and that is where the fuel went! In the heat of the moment, I still remembered the dangers of proximity between radio equipment and flammable liquid. Parking the radio mic, I grabbed an extinguisher and thankfully for Andrew and me nothing ignited. All this was to my advantage as I had bet him a bottle of wine he couldn't do a 49 second lap, which I had just achieved. He only managed 50.1, even though he thought he was on fire.

The Tornado Bomber run! Live from the cockpit and hooked up by Garry Stagg and Martin Hobson – take a bow.

Locked out: Heading out of the box to the toilet while commentating solo and the door lock wasn't on the "snib" – fatal error.

Power: Picture the scene, Wednesday night stock cars, I'm in the sun-kissed box, it's warm, busy with great racing and I lean back on the high comms box chair thinking life can't get any better. My knee hits the master power off button and the system shuts down. The panic was real!

The interviews: I simply should have kept a list. Pick a star in UK racing and we have had them on air. Even many global giants of the sport. It's all for Garry in my eyes, it was his baby, he pushed me to go out of my comfort zone and helped me become the broadcaster I am today. He still listens in to every broadcast we do from the Garry Stagg Commentary Tower. Beautiful.

Chapter 16: Tales From the Tower   245

Right: An early interview for Duncan with Jet Pack Man.

Below: Duncan enthusiastically interviews World Saloon Car star Gabriele Tarquini at the first Super Touring event in 2015.

The Knockhill commentary team have chosen their two all-time favourite competitors, Niall Mackenzie and Gordon Shedden. Here are their top ten memories of Knockhill.

Below: A young Tarran Mackenzie tastes early success at Knockhill.

Niall Mackenzie

Niall Mackenzie's life with Knockhill goes back forty-three years and his track record on two wheels is exceptional, having risen from the Knockhill club scene to racing nationally, becoming a successful Grand Prix rider before returning to win the British Superbike Championship three times. He came out of retirement a couple of times to race at Knockhill and now oversees the racing exploits of his two sons as well as running the Niall Mackenzie Superbike Experience at Knockhill. Niall is the first president of the Knockhill Motor Sports Club and is a regular at trackside, helping promote the sport at all levels.

Here are Niall's top ten Knockhill memories

1981 First-ever career win on my beloved Yamaha RD350LC.

1993 Riding my GP 500cc Valvoline ROC Yamaha to victory at the Jock Taylor Trophy Memorial meeting.

1996 BSB double win on the Cadburys Boost Yamaha having been pushed hard by James Whitham.

1998 BSB double win after fending off Troy Bayliss and the late great Steve Hislop.

2015 Tarran Mac's first-ever Superstock 600 class win at BSB.

2016 Tarran Mac's first-ever British Supersport class win at BSB.

2017 Winning the Yamaha Pro-Am revival race at the ripe age of fifty-six.

2019 Tarran Mac pushing Scott Redding to a second position in BSB.

2020 Taylor Mac dominating in the wet Superstock 1000 class.

2021 Taylor Mac dominating in the dry Superstock 1000 class.

Above: A proud dad! Niall pictured with sons Taylor and Tarran (left) with Derek Butcher's sons Jamie and Rory (right).

Below: Niall rounds McIntyre's during an anti-clockwise race meeting.

Right: The eyes on the prize! Father and son Niall and Taylor study the opposition.

Opposite, top left: The eyes have it! A picture of concentration with Tarran.

Opposite, top right: Taylor at speed on a wet BSB round.

Opposite, bottom: TT Legend John McGuinness and Niall share a laugh on a Honda C90 that was travelling from Land's End to John O'Groats in 2020.

Chapter 16: Tales From the Tower 249

Above: Always a showman. Gordon flies the flag during an Edinburgh city centre promo on Castle Terrace while hanging out of his Touring Car in 2009.

Right: A sicteen-year-old Gordon becomes one of Knockhill's instructing team – who knew back then what the future would hold.

Bottom: A sign of things to come as Gordon is already learning to "fly" over the Knockhill kerbs!

Opposite. top: Doing his bit for the promotion of road safety in Scotland just before driving his BTCC car over the Forth Road Bridge.

Opposite, middle: A heavy landing about to happen at the chicane!

Opposite, bottom: A race winner from the outset as a young Gordon picks up yet another trophy in the Ford Credit Fiesta Championship.

Gordon Shedden

Gordon Shedden made his racing debut at Knockhill in a Scottish Ford Fiesta XR2 at the age of seventeen before racing nationally in a Fiesta, progressed to a SEAT Cupra before taking the BTCC by storm with Honda, becoming the first Scot to win the coveted title three times. He ventured into World Touring Cars with Audi and has competed in almost anything with four wheels, usually winning! He has also featured as a guest driver on BBC's *Top Gear* and many other programmes and has won top awards in the historic scene, adding many titles to his illustrious saloon car racing career.

Here are Gordon's top ten Knockhill memories

1994 First visit with my dad to BTCC when Tarquini rolled the Alfa Romeo.

1995 Started instructing when sixteen years old.

1998 First Ford XR2 win in second ever race.

2000 Win in TOCA Fiesta race (red car).

2001 BTCC (unofficial) debut win in Production class Ford Focus.

2005 Podium in Porsche Cup celebrity car.

2006 BTCC podium in debut year with Honda Integra, the same weekend as flying in Tornado from Leuchars.

2009 Edinburgh Castle parade.

2014 Forth Bridge crossings with Jim Clark Cortina.

2007 Onwards! Wins in 2007, 2010, 2011, 2015.

Chapter 16: Tales From the Tower

Top: Gordon got to go subsonic over the North Sea in a Tornado in 2006, courtesy of the RAF at Leuchars.

Bottom: That winning feeling. Gordon has been a multiple winner at Knockhill from 2007 onwards.

Acknowledgements and Image Credits

I would like to thank all the photographers, both known and unknown, from the Knockhill archive who have submitted their work for this publication. The photos really help to tell the story of how both the venue and the business of Knockhill have evolved over the five decades. I would like to thank my colleagues for their input and the entire team at Black & White Publishing, especially Thomas Ross, for his dedication and support in pulling the book together; also Campbell and Ali for their belief in commissioning it. I hope everyone enjoys reading the book, but more so, admiring the many special and memorable images within.

Alex Griffin: 230 (middle left)

Alex Ireland: 129 (top), 130 (top), 138 (top), 225, 228 (top)

Archie Love: 77, 81 (middle), 81 (bottom), 84 (top), 86 (bottom), 90, 92, 101, 106, 109, 113 (bottom), 122 (bottom), 125, 181 (bottom), 191 (top row), 192, 193 (top), 196 (bottom left), 203 (bottom right), 219 (bottom), 234 (top), 248 (top)

Ashleigh Morris: 197 (bottom right)

Cameron Robb: 135 (bottom), 223 (top)

culture-images GmbH / Alamy Stock Photo: viii

Dan Jess: 7-8, 13 (right), 14, 15 (top), 17, 22 (top left), 26 (bottom), 27-28, 52-53, 54 (top), 55, 70 (bottom), 78 (bottom), 83, 85, 93, 102-103, 105 (bottom), 114 (top), 138 (bottom), 248 (bottom right)

Derek Butcher: 18 (all apart from middle right)

Derek Horne: 75 (bottom), 108 (bottom), 227 (bottom right)

Derek Weir: 61, 79 (top)

Double Red: ix (right), 180 (top right), 181 (top right), 183 (top), 185 (top row), 187 (top left), 217 (bottom left), 247, 249 (top row)

Duncan Vincent: 183 (bottom right), 243 (left)

Eddie Kelly Motorsport Photography: 153, 199 (top)

ESP Media: 32 (top), 36

Flat Out Photography: 111, 131, 132 (bottom), 183 (bottom left), 193 (bottom row), 196 (top), 200 (top), 205 (bottom), 213 (top), 215 (top left), 224, 227 (middle), 228 (middle left), 229, 240, 243 (right), 251 (middle)

FPNW Photography: 139

Frank Love: xvii (bottom), 57-58, 218 (bottom)

Garry Stagg: 220 (bottom), 221 (top)

Gary Stevenson: 228 (middle right)

Gemma Hobbs: 237 (left)

Gordon Shedden: 41

Iain Nicolson: 15 (bottom four), 16 (top), 59, 66-67, 70 (top), 75 (top), 78 (top)

Ian Cochrane: 226 (3rd row left)

Jakob Ebrey Photography: 23 (left), 40 (top), 71, 80, 112, 113 (top), 196 (bottom right), 215 (top right, bottom), 251 (top), 252 (bottom)

Jakob Ebrey Photography / Jeff Bloxham: 241

James Sansun: 226 (top left)

Jeff Bloxham: 12, 197 (top), 50 (top)

Jim Maguire: 226 (2nd top left), 228 (bottom)

Jim Moir: x, xii, xiv, xvi, xvii (top), 10-11, 13 (left), 16 (bottom right), 23 (right), 24 (bottom), 25, 31, 33-35, 37, 38 (bottom), 40 (bottom), 44-49, 50 (bottom), 51, 54 (bottom), 56, 60, 65 (top), 74, 87, 94-95, 100, 104, 115 (bottom), 116 (top), 119-120, 122 (top), 123 (bottom), 129 (bottom), 136-137, 143, 149, 156-168, 186 (top row), 197 (bottom left), 198 (bottom), 199 (bottom), 200 (bottom), 211, 217 (top), 219 (top), 238 (top), 250 (top, bottom), 251 (bottom)

John Fife: ix (left)

John Leitch: 68

Jon Bolton: 231 (bottom)

Kenny Hilton: 216 (bottom)

Kensington Palace: 141 (bottom), 146 (top), 220 (top)

Knockhill Archives: xi, 3, 5, 19-21, 38 (top), 82 (both), 88-89, 189, 232

Lewis Haughton: 148, 223 (bottom)

Mhairi Ligertwood: 227 (bottom left)

Motorsport Images / Jeff Bloxham: 98-99

Neil Smith: 226 (bottom)

Paul McGinnes: 230 (top)

Porsche GB: 147 (top)

Power Images: vi, 1, 39, 42-43, 114 (bottom), 116 (bottom), 118 (bottom), 126-127, 128, 130 (bottom), 133-134, 135 (top), 141 (top), 144, 147 (bottom), 152, 154-155, 180 (bottom), 184 (top row, middle), 185 (bottom), 186 (bottom), 187 (top right), 188 (bottom), 190 (top), 191 (bottom), 194-195, 202 (bottom), 203 (bottom left), 204 (top row), 212, 214 (top), 217 (bottom right), 221 (bottom), 233, 234 (bottom), 236, 239 (bottom), 242 (top), 245 (bottom), 246 (bottom), 254

Ronnie Weir: xiii (top), 18 (middle right), 22 (bottom), 62-64, 65 (bottom), 79 (bottom), 86 (top), 198 (top, middle), 248 (bottom left)

Scott Dickson: 222 (top)

Scott Footman: 132 (top), 210 (top)

Sean Garswood: 226 (3rd row right)

Shana Cheyne: 230 (bottom right)

Steven Mackay: 169-178, 242 (bottom), 245 (top)

Stevie McCann: 150-151

Stuart Gray: 4, 24 (top), 26 (top right), 29-30, 32 (bottom), 81 (top), 84 (bottom), 96, 110, 118 (top), 123 (top), 140, 146 (bottom), 181 (top left), 182 (top), 184 (bottom), 187 (bottom), 188 (top), 201, 202 (top, middle), 203 (top row), 204 (bottom), 205 (top), 208-209, 210 (bottom), 214 (bottom), 216 (top), 218 (top), 249 (bottom), 250 (middle), 237 (right)

Stuart Moss: 230 (bottom left)

Team Dynamics: 252 (top)

Tom Brown: 22 (top right), 72, 91, 108 (top), 115 (top), 179, 180 (top left), 182 (bottom), 213 (bottom)

V9 Photoworks: 117, 190 (bottom), 206-207, 222 (bottom), 226 (top right), 227 (top), 231 (top), 246 (top)

Over 50 years since its building, Knockhill has grown to become Scotland's National Motorsport Centre and is host to the UK's top televised motorsport car and bike events. The circuit is situated just 30 minutes from Edinburgh, 40 miles from Glasgow and 2 hours from Aberdeen. Knockhill is a truly versatile venue and the perfect choice for all events including corporate days, team building, karting, trackdays and exciting driving experiences.

Our Venue

Knockhill is Scotland's only accredited FIA and MSA approved venue! With extensive and ongoing investment in our facilities we are able to provide new and exciting experiences and racing events that are rivalled by no other. Our famous 1.27 mile long circuit, hillside rally stage, 4x4 off road track, 500m outdoor karting circuit, skid pan, restaurants and conferencing facilities continue to form our unique venue.

Our Team

This is surely one of our finest assets and always a hot topic with our customers! We strive to provide the best possible experiences and our skilled team plays an important part in delivering these. Everyone – from our ground staff, instructors, sales team and directors – is friendly, approachable, correctly qualified and passionate about their role at Knockhill. We all look forward to welcoming you to Knockhill.

www.knockhill.com

Facebook: Knockhill Racing Circuit
Twitter: @krcircuit
Instagram: @knockhillracingcircuit